This book examines the central questions concerning the duty to obey the law: the meaning of this duty; whether and where it should be acknowledged; whether and when it should be disregarded. Many contemporary philosophers deny the very existence of this duty, but take a cautious stance toward political disobedience. This "toothless anarchism," Professor Gans argues, should be discarded in favor of a converse position confirming the existence of a duty to obey the law which can and should be easily outweighed by values and principles of political morality.

Informed by the Israeli experience of political disobedience motivated by radically differing moral outlooks, the author sets out the principles which should guide our attitude to law and political authority even amidst clashing ideologies and irreconcilable moralities. This book will be of interest to students and scholars of law, philosophy and politics, and anyone concerned with the individual's responsibilities toward his or her political community.

DATE DUE FOR RETURN

PHILOSOPHICAL ANARCHISM AND POLITICAL DISOBEDIENCE

PHILOSOPHICAL ANARCHISM AND POLITICAL DISOBEDIENCE

CHAIM GANS

Faculty of Law, Tel Aviv University

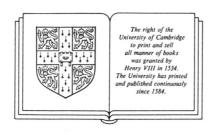

CAMBRIDGE UNIVERSITY PRESS

Cambridge

New York   Port Chester

Melbourne   Sydney

Published by the Press Syndicate of the University of Cambridge
The Pitt Building, Trumpington Street, Cambridge CB2 IRP
40 West 20th Street, New York, NY 10011-4211, USA
10 Stamford Road, Oakleigh, Victoria 3166, Australia

First published 1992

Printed in Great Britain at the University Press, Cambridge

A catalogue record for this book is available from the British Library

Library of Congress cataloguing in publication data
Gans, Chaim.
Philosophical anarchism and political disobedience / Chaim Gans.
p. cm.
ISBN 0 521 41450 4
1. Civil disobedience. 2. Anarchism. 3. Criticism (Philosophy)
I. Title.
JC328.3.G35 1992
323.6'5'01–d020 92-27373 CIP

ISBN 0 521 41450 4 hardback

To the memory of my mother
Yehudit Gans

Contents

Preface

While writing this book, I moved between two types of interests and audiences with which I sense a connection: between political involvement and academic work, between the Israeli public and the community of Anglo-American philosophers. The former served mainly to feed my passions and supply my project with an urgent sense of purpose. The latter provided it with tradition, tools, discipline and tone.

For a few consecutive years during the early eighties I dealt with the duty to obey the law in several courses I taught at Tel Aviv University. The books and articles comprising my syllabus expressed a position on which an almost total consensus had been consolidated among philosophers during the seventies. According to this position there is no duty to obey the law, mainly because none of the arguments offered in its support proves it to be universally applicable. Though I agreed then and still agree with many of the details of this position, it nonetheless troubled me. My discomfort stemmed mainly from the disintegrative reading of the arguments for the duty to obey criticized by those holding the view in question; from the unnecessarily strict construal of the concept of generic duties which the position presupposes; and from the embarrassing gap between the radical look of this thesis and the tameness of its practical implications. I was also bothered by the absence of a rigorous discussion of the conclusions on the limits of the duty to obey, following from its particular grounds.

Several years ago, I attempted to write an article for an anthology whose publication was initiated by the "Yesh Gvul" ("There's a Limit") movement, an Israeli movement of the conscientious objectors to the war in Lebanon in 1982–4 and those refusing to serve in the territories occupied by Israel since 1967. I envisioned an audience of Israeli public figures, jurists and journalists. Most of these, much like their colleagues anywhere else, tend to repeat in their public statements the common wisdom that citizens, especially of democracies, have a right to disagree with the law but must not disobey it. I found myself trying to seek out and dig up the prolific roots of this weed.

My article for the anthology was never completed. I was forced into a 'discussion on a different scale from that of an article by my dissatisfaction with quite a number of components of the contemporary philosophical literature on the duty to obey the law, and by my wish to make sure that the angers I felt at the prevailing position on this duty among publicists and politicians were justified ones.

These angers had originated in autobiographical sources. In the early seventies I had spent over three years of my military service in the Gaza strip. During this period I felt much conscientious unrest. I was torn between my deep commitment to Israel on the one hand, and my objection to its ruling the Palestinians on the other; between my Zionist upbringing and my fear for Zionism's integrity; as a result I did not oppose my stationing in Gaza altogether, but at the same time resisted obeying selectively many of the orders of my commanding officers. When Israel further entrenched its rule over the occupied territories at the end of the seventies, officially adopting the settlement ideology of "Gush Emunim" – the political avant-garde of Israel's right wing and Israeli nationalism – I considered it appropriate to object totally to serving my reserve military duty within the mechanism dominating the Palestinians.

I was, of course, not the first to do so, and since the 1987 onset of the Palestinian uprising in the occupied territories many more have followed; not enough, however. One of the reasons for this is the continuous campaign waged by journalists and politicians against conscientious objection and political refusal to serve in the occupied territories. Philosophical writing (this book will also be published in Hebrew) cannot of itself provide a swift answer to such campaigns. Although it is unfortunate that political events in the Middle East move slowly, this does at least leave room for the equally slow influences of philosophical contemplation.

I received the aid and support of many people in the course of my work. My deepest debt of gratitude is to my friend Meir Dan-Cohen, for his comments on the drafts of the first, second and fourth chapters and his untiring encouragement. Ronald Dworkin read an early version of the first two chapters, and Joseph Raz read a similar version of the third one as well. Both offered a great many illuminating remarks, but my debt to them extends far beyond these. Both of them supervised my previous major philosophical effort – my doctoral dissertation at Oxford. I then learned more philosophy from them than I have from anyone else, and I assume that much of this, though probably not enough, has filtered through into the present book too.

I received comments on the first two chapters from Kenneth Campbell, Ruth Gavison, Andrei Marmor and Ariel Porat. Drafts of the second chapter were also read and remarked on by Miri Gur-Arieh, Amir Horowitz and Igor Primoratz. Lucian Bebchuck made many important comments on an early version of the fourth chapter. Portions of a Hebrew version of the first chapter were published in article form in *Mishpatim* 17 (1987), 507. Portions of an early Hebrew version of the second chapter were also published in *Mishpatim* 17 (1987), 353. At the time, many useful comments were offered by the editors. A nearly identical version of the third chapter was published in the *Oxford Journal of Legal Studies* 8 (1988), 920. Also, an early Hebrew version of the fourth chapter was published in the *Tel Aviv University Law Review* 13 (1988), 359. In this case too, members of the editorial board made many important remarks. I am grateful for permission to use these articles.

The dual audience to which I addressed myself as I wrote also caused me to move between Hebrew and English. I am grateful to Rela Mazali for the sensitivity she has shown to my Hebrew mood and the precision with which she has rendered the details of my arguments in translating the present version. I am also indebted to Dori Kimmel for the freshness and enthusiasm with which he provided me in assisting preparation of the footnotes and bibliography. Adi Ayal joined in at the last stage in preparing the index. The Zegla Institute for Comparative Law at the Tel Aviv University Faculty of law offered me financial aid. I would like to thank Professor Daniel Friedman, Director of the Institute, and his fellow members of the board for their generosity.

Tel Aviv, February, 1991

Introduction

This is a book about the central questions concerning the duty to obey the law: about the meaning of this duty; whether and where it should be acknowledged; and whether and when it should be disregarded. An extensive store of answers to these questions has been accumulating on the shelves of philosophy ever since the Socratic *Apology* and *Crito*. The war in Vietnam, the American missiles positioned on European ground and the opposition aroused by both, have caused many Anglo-American philosophers to air out these answers in the course of the last two decades. They have re-examined the basic theoretical questions pertaining to the meaning and justification of this duty, and offered significant innovations on the more practical applicational questions of the duty's limits and the desirable ways of disregarding it.

Several lineaments characterize the position dominant among contemporary philosophers on the question of the duty to obey. This position is one of philosophical anarchism. It amounts to a denial of the very existence of a duty to obey the state. However, those maintaining this position adopt a careful attitude towards political disobedience, and refrain from justifying overly frequent performance of such violations. Finally, their treatment of political disobedience draws upon a background of humanist–liberal morality, a morality widely accepted by Western society which can consequently be taken for granted. They believe it right to disobey the law sometimes for value-based reasons, but the values they accept as justifications for such disobedience are humanistic ones.

In this book, I shall depart somewhat from these characteristics. First, the theory of the limits of the duty to obey that I shall suggest will, in its basic structure, be a formal one. It will accordingly be free of substantive moral values, humanistic or otherwise. Second, I shall recommend a liberal attitude towards morally based disobedience. I shall contend that the moral duty to obey the law is, for the most part, a duty not to disobey it for a-moral reasons (considerations of self-interest, for example, or of economic efficiency). It is almost never a duty to avoid disobeying the law for moral reasons. Finally, I shall argue that within our correct attitude towards law and state, a carefully qualified duty to obey them should be acknowledged. The practical consequences of this stance will not differ greatly from those of the one currently prevalent among philosophers, which, as stated, is a position denying the existence of this duty. However, the formulation I shall propose has some important theoretical advantages which I shall point out in due course.

There are two prominent foundations for contemporary philosophers' denial of the duty to obey the law. According to one, it follows from the very meaning of this duty, that its acknowledgment entails a surrender of moral autonomy. A moral obligation involving such a surrender is a contradiction in terms. Thus, according to this line of thought, such an obligation is logically impossible. I have termed this form of the denial of the duty to obey "autonomy-based anarchism." In the first chapter of this book, which discusses the meaning of the duty to obey, I will also deal with this form of anarchism. However, rather than dealing with it of itself, much of the chapter sets out to clarify various inadequately analyzed components of the duty to obey, components which lead many to conceive of it as involving a surrender of autonomy. As I will show, these components do not, in the end, entail such a surrender, and accordingly autonomy-based anarchism is mistaken.

The second reason why many contemporary philosophers deny the duty to obey the law arises from their criticism of various attempts undertaken throughout the history of the subject to ground the duty to obey. There are six central attempts of this type. One is based on gratitude, another on consent, a third on the negative consequences of disobeying the law, a fourth on fairness and a fifth on the duty to support just institutions. A sixth justification has been proposed only recently and it is based on communal obligations.

Many philosophers are of the opinion that the first five attempts listed above fail to ground the duty to obey. The last, most recently offered basis has not yet been discussed in the literature, but the reasoning of some of the criticism directed at the other proposals applies here too. The denial of the duty to obey the law which is based on a rejection of its grounds is termed "critical anarchism" here. The second chapter will examine these grounds carefully and blunt the edge of such anarchism in more than one way.

The third chapter has two objectives. The first is to make it clear that the justifications for the duty to obey discussed in the previous chapter do not apply unless certain conditions are met. These conditions pertain to the degree of morality and justness shown by the political and legal systems. The chapter's second objective is the presentation of additional arguments for the duty to obey, which pertain particularly to democratic political systems and turn upon the fairness and participation characteristics of democracy. The third chapter thus combines two separate topics; that of the conditions under which the justifications for the duty to obey do or do not apply, and that of democracy as an additional source of justifications for the duty to obey. I combine the two, chiefly, due to the need for emphasizing democracy's twofold effect upon the duty to obey the law. For those who believe in it, it forms a basis for this duty. Yet, inasmuch as it constitutes the governmental manifestation of a humanistic conception of justice, it is also a prerequisite for the applicability of the duty's other foundations, those discussed in the second chapter.

Given the meaning of the duty to obey discussed in the first chapter, and its justifications and conditions of application discussed in the second and third, a complete theory of this duty will require an answer to one further, significant question: the question of its limits. The answer to this question will occupy the book's fourth and final chapter. As stated above, Anglo-American philosophers' treatment of this question presupposes that a humanistic code of values can simply be taken for granted. The present discussion was composed in Israel. Here, it is difficult to take a humanistic morality for granted. The last two decades have seen disobedience and further infringement upon the duty to obey, aimed not only against policies that contradict the humanistic conception of justice. True, these too have occurred. Some acts of nonconsent have been (and are still) carried out on the basis of a humanistic morality. This is the case as regards the refusal of many soldiers to serve during the war in Lebanon, between 1982 and 1984, as they considered it unjust, and the refusal of many to serve in the West Bank and Gaza due to the unjustness they ascribe to Israel's continued reign in these territories and its oppression of the Palestinian nation. However, Israel has also witnessed disobedience based on nationalistic and religious conceptions of justice. In 1978 Israel signed a peace treaty with Egypt. Its terms specified Israel's evacuation of the Sinai peninsula and the Raffah Gap, which it had occupied since the Six-Day War. Many Israelis considered the evacuation of the Raffah Gap injurious to national values. They deemed this reason enough to disobey the orders of the Israeli government intended to fulfill Israel's side of the agreement, i.e. the evacuation of the Raffah Gap. Another instance of this type of disobedience had to do with a policy adhered to by the Israeli government until 1977, that of non-settlement in the parts of the West Bank that were densely populated by Arabs. This policy entailed non-settlement in areas that are viewed through Jewish biblical history as some of the most important in the Land of Israel. It thus infringed upon the basic values of Israeli nationalism. The Israeli fundamentalists, the members of Gush Emunim, broke the laws that upheld this policy. They disobeyed the government and settled at Kadum, near Nablus, capital of Samaria's dense Arab population.

Can the duty to obey the law be understood and justified in a manner allowing for its violation on the grounds of both humanistic values and values of nationalism? My discussions, in the first three chapters, of the meaning of the duty to obey and its justifications will enable me to answer this question in the affirmative in the fourth and last chapter. Of the arguments that vault the hurdles of anarchist criticism, at least two will be fundamentally humanistic: the fairness argument and the democratic one. The limits of the duty to obey deriving from these will consequently accommodate only a disobedience that is based on humanistic values. However, at least one of the arguments that vaults these hurdles, the one based on the negative consequences of disobeying the law, is compatible with any political morality whatsoever, regardless of its values. The limits of obedience that I shall try to elicit from this basis will be formal ones, independent of any humanistic conception of justice. They will consequently accommodate a disobedience founded not only on humanistic values, but also on any values whatsoever, whatever their contents.

The possibility of outlining formal boundaries for the duty to obey the law, boundaries totally devoid of substantive values, will be the final chord of a motif that is central in this book. This motif consists of underlining the secondary status of the duty to obey the law, relative to other moral duties, emphasizing its inherent dependence upon the substantive values of political morality.

CHAPTER I

The meaning of the duty to obey the law and autonomy-based anarchism

I. MORAL OBLIGATION, POLITICAL OBLIGATION AND THE RULE OF LAW

[handwritten margin note: should be a moral question]

There is no point in posing the question whether the law must be obeyed as a legal one. Legal questions are questions whose answers are provided by the law. Were the law to answer the question whether or not it must be obeyed, the question of the duty to obey would simply pop up again, as one might then question the duty to obey the law that had answered this question. The duty to obey the law should thus be understood as an extra-legal duty. As such it can be understood in many different ways. For instance, it can be construed as pertaining to personal interests or national ones, as a religious duty or a moral one. I shall treat it here as a moral duty. This, I think, is also the attitude taken towards it in the many public contexts that employ it as a tool for preaching and chastisement. When politicians, journalists and public figures wish, at any point, to prod us into actions whose performance is ordained by law, their advice never comes from the standpoint of our personal interests. Neither do they inform us of our religious duties. And when referring to the duty to obey the law as a national one, they do so in the belief that it is morality that requires, justifies, or at least allows for the service of national interests.

The question of the moral duty to obey the law is a question about obeying the laws of human societies. I understand the concept of law here as it is understood within the tradition of Legal Positivism. According to this theory, norms and rules need not meet any moral conditions whatsoever in order to count as laws in the legal sense. Norms and rules are laws if, and only if, they fulfill a list of certain *factual* conditions (e.g. having been enacted according to the appropriate procedure by a legislative body or its authorized agent, or having been rulings of the courts, etc.). It is worthwhile dealing with the issue of the duty to obey on the background of the positivist conception of law as this allows for the possibility of asking whether there is a moral duty to obey immoral laws. (Apparently, this question is also left open, or is at least viewed as such, under a Natural Law conception of law. Natural Law is traditionally thought to rule out the very legality of immoral laws. It thus pulls the rug out from under the possibility of having any opportunity to obey immoral laws. Nevertheless, Thomas Aquinas, the classical theorist of Natural Law, believed that unjust laws were sometimes to be obeyed to "avoid scandal and disturbance."[1])

The duty to obey the law addressed by this book is the ordinary citizen's duty to obey. This must be distinguished from the authorities' duty to obey, which constitutes part of the value of the rule of law. There is good reason for considering the subjects' duty to obey to be part of the issue of the rule of law. First, the literal meaning of the term "the rule of law" includes the subjects' obedience.[2] (Disobedience on their part means an only partial rule of law.) Second, part of the considerations favoring the authorities' obedience to the law, considerations some of which I shall discuss immediately, are identical to those justifying the subjects' obedience.

However, despite these reasons for confusing the two, there are even stronger reasons for distinguishing between them. First, the authorities, unlike the citizens, owe more to the rule of law than mere obedience. For the law to rule, the legislative authorities, for instance, must not only obey it but also avoid retroactive or contradictory legislation, refrain from acutely controversial legislation, word their laws clearly, publicize them, etc.[3] To fulfill their task in creating the rule of law, the judiciary, for instance, must be equally accessible to all, keep the rules of natural justice, explain their decisions, etc.[4] In other words, the idea of a rule of law demands the authorities' discipline on a much wider range of topics than mere obedience. Of subjects it demands obedience only.

The second reason for the distinction made above is much more pertinent to the present discussion. It has to do with the fundamental

---

[1] St. Thomas Aquinas, *Summa Theologica* (London: Blackfriars, 1966), Part 2, Question XCVI, 4th Article (vol. 28, p. 129).

[2] See also Joseph Raz, *The Authority of Law* (Oxford: Oxford University Press, 1979), p. 212.

[3] For a detailed discussion see Lon L. Fuller, *The Morality of Law*, revised edition (New Haven: Yale University Press, 1969), ch. 2; John Rawls, *A Theory of Justice* (Cambridge, Mass.: Harvard University Press, 1971), pp. 235–43; Raz, *The Authority of Law*, pp. 214–19.

[4] *Ibid.*

difference between the importance of obedience on the part of the authorities and the importance of the ordinary subject's duty to obey the law. This difference stems from two sources. First, some of the considerations supporting the authorities' obedience are completely irrelevant to the question of the subjects' obedience. These have to do with the principle of the separation of powers. Were the authorities entrusted with the roles of bringing to trial, judging and carrying out the courts' rulings, to disobey the law, or in other words fail to enforce it or fail to punish its violators, it would be in place to ask just who determines society's conduct – these authorities or the government and the legislature. This question doesn't arise at all when an ordinary subject disobeys the law and is duly punished. Second, although some considerations support obedience on the part of both subjects and authorities, their cogency as regards the latter is infinitely greater. A central consideration of this type is discussed in detail in the second chapter. It relates to the negative consequences of disobedience for the legal system's role as a tool for establishing and enforcing the conduct appropriate to and within society. This consideration supports obedience on the part of both subjects and authorities, but its potency within the context of the latter can hardly be exaggerated. In the first place, disobedience on the part of the authorities occurs within view of the public eye. More important, however, is the existence of a remedy for subjects' violations, where almost no such remedy exists for any damage caused by the authorities' disobedience. Subjects who disobey the law may either be forced to obey it or punished for their disobedience. In most cases no one is there to force the authorities to obey. No one is there to punish them either.

The practice assigning the concept of the rule of law to the authorities' duties only is common among many legal and political thinkers.[5] Such authors draw a distinction, or at least assume one, between the rule of law and the subjects' duty to obey, though as stated the literal meaning of "the rule of law" can contain this duty. *to obey* Ignorance of this distinction is a central source of prevalent exaggerations of the importance of the ordinary subject's duty to obey, and of other serious misconceptions as to the limits of this duty. As will be shown in the course of this book, I do not intend to disclaim the importance of this duty. I merely wish to claim that many worthy

---

[5] See Raz, *The Authority of Law*, p. 212; Fuller, *The Morality of Law*, ch. 2; Rawls, *A Theory of Justice*, pp. 235–43.

contenders exaggerate its importance and misunderstand its limits, mainly because they confuse it with the rule of law.

Anglo-American writers usually identify the duty to obey the law with what they call political obligation. This last has to do with the "good citizen" concept, that of the citizen who plays his or her part in the support and defense of his country and its institutions. Two points raised by such equations deserve some elaboration. For one thing, obeying the law is only one possible means of expressing good citizenship. Some accordingly conclude that political obligation is a wider, more inclusive notion than the duty to obey the law.[6] This position should be examined. The second point concerns the tone of intimacy cast over the duty to obey the law, through discussion of the relationship between citizen and country. Several comments on this intimacy are called for.

As regards the first point: true, good citizenship can be expressed through channels other than obedience to the law. One can do much more for her or his country's institutions than merely obey their orders. It is possible, for instance, to contribute to one's country's treasury more than one's due according to the tax laws. One can serve in the army for longer than the term specified by the relevant laws. However, it is doubtful whether there is any point in discussing these and similar acts as part of political *obligation*. If any values exist that justify this duty (a question I shall address in the second chapter), then a distinction should be drawn between actions whose performance is in some sense (discussed below) necessary in the service of these values, actions which are thus considered duties, and actions that further these values but lie *beyond the call of duty*.[7] Surely, the actions ensuring a necessary minimum for the furtherance of such values must be classified as the duties that serve them. Obeying the law is an action that meets this condition. As the second chapter shall illustrate, it constitutes a minimum requirement, necessary for the existence of a society. It naturally doesn't follow from this that other types of action cannot be seen as constituting parts of political obligation. We shall find, however, that obeying the law (within the limits to be specified by this book) is the central and most solid core of this obligation.

Obeying the law relates to good citizenship in much the same way

---

[6] See e.g. A. J. Simmons, *Moral Principles and Political Obligations* (Princeton: Princeton University Press, 1979), p. 5.

[7] On the moral category of actions beyond the call of duty, see David Heyd, *Supererogation – Its Status in Ethical Theory* (Cambridge: Cambridge University Press, 1982).

that refraining from manslaughter relates to the sanctity of human life. The value of sanctity may be facilitated in various ways besides refraining from manslaughter, through various types of lifesaving deeds. Though these clearly serve the value in question, we don't conceive of them, at least not of all of them, as part of the duty founded on it. It is arguable whether or not specific kinds of lifesaving deeds, of the good Samaritan type for instance, constitute duties in the service of this value. Obviously, however, not all lifesaving deeds will count as such. Equally obviously, avoiding manslaughter, the bare minimum necessary for the value's realization, forms the solid core of the duty that serves it. A similar relationship exists between the values of good citizenship and obeying the law. The values of good citizenship may be facilitated in many ways besides merely obeying the law. Deeds such as additional army service or enlarged payments to the treasury clearly further them as well. However, as the next chapters will show, and subject to the reservations they expound, obeying the law forms the minimum necessary for the furtherance of these values; the hard core of the duty that serves them. Even if it is the case that political obligation includes more than just obeying the law, obeying the law still constitutes its hard core. I shall accordingly treat the two as equivalents throughout.

A second point is intimated by this identification of the duty to obey the law with political obligation and the values of good citizenship. This equation casts the duty to obey as a duty towards the laws of the community to which one belongs. Some claim that the duty to obey has to do with the specific relationship between the individual and her or his community; that it is the individual's duty to the laws of her or his country only, the country of which he or she is a citizen, and not to the laws of other countries.[8] This claim is too strong. True, if there is a duty to obey the law it is, first and foremost, a duty to obey the laws of the land in which each of us lives. Yet it is not a duty to obey these laws alone. I believe this last claim of mine to be consistent with what people conceive of as the duty to obey. As the second chapter will show,[9] it is also consistent with the series of considerations supporting this duty. Some of these (the principle of fairness and especially communal obligations) indeed support it as a

---

[8] See Simmons, *Moral Principles and Political Obligations*, pp. 30–5; Ronald Dworkin, *Law's Empire* (Cambridge, Mass.: Harvard University Press, 1986), pp. 193, 199; A. M. Honore, "Must We Obey? Necessity as a Ground of Obligation," *Virginia Law Review* 67 (1981), 39, pp. 39, 47; Joseph Raz, *The Morality of Freedom* (Oxford: Oxford University Press, 1986), p. 105.   [9] See pp. 81–3; 87–9 below.

duty specifically owed by individuals to their communities. Others (the argument from the consequences of disobedience and the duty to support just institutions) are not limited to this specific manifestation of the duty to obey. However, they still apply, for the most part, to the individual–community relation, as people have the most occasion to implement these considerations with regard to the laws of their own countries.[10] In short, the duty to obey the law discussed in the course of this book is mainly, but not exclusively, the individual's duty to the political community within which he or she lives. It is a duty that forms the innermost core of the individual's duty towards her or his community. As I have already stated, I construe this duty as a moral one, applying to ordinary subjects.

2. MORAL AUTONOMY AND THE RIGID CONCEPTION OF THE DUTY TO OBEY

As some would have it, the moral duty to obey the law entails, by virtue of the concept's very meaning, a constant willingness to perform whatever the law says, while surrendering one's judgment of either its contents or the conditions of its application. Others hold a position which is less extreme, but is nonetheless quite rigid too. They construe the duty to obey as compatible with an evaluation of the law and even with an explicit critique of it, but believe it incompatible with any breach of it that might stem from such evaluations.[11]

Under both these rigid readings, the duty to obey becomes a problematic concept. On the assumption that laws are capable of generating damage to values that are more important than the ones served by this duty, it emerges here as contradictory to the principle of moral autonomy. It is this principle that forms the very core of moral action and moral responsibility. Anyone bound by moral duties has, according to the principle of autonomy, a duty and a right

---

[10] According to Dworkin, *Law's Empire*, p. 191 and Simmons, *Moral Principles and Political Obligations*, p. 33, this fact is unsuccessful in clarifying the intimacy of the unique duty owed by citizens specifically to the laws of their country. Were this the only explanation for the fact that the duty to obey is specific to the relationship between citizen and country, Simmons and Dworkin might be correct. However, as stated in the text, some of the grounds for the duty to obey support it, initially, as an intimate duty owed by citizens to their country. I shall return to this issue in the second chapter.

[11] For a list of those adhering to the view that acknowledging authority involves one of the above forms of willingness, and for complex discussions of some of the aspects of the concept of authority entailing the need to understand it as involving them, see R. E. Flathman, *The Practice of Political Authority* (Chicago: Chicago University Press, 1980), ch. 5; Raz, *The Authority of Law*, ch. 3.

to act consistently with their better judgment and with all relevant considerations. The acts a person performs are considered her or his own, not other people's. He or she is held responsible for them. Yet how is this possible with regard to actions in the context of which they are required not to weigh or act upon considerations which they may deem relevant?

Furthermore, we have no foreknowledge of the future conditions under which given laws will apply or of the contents of laws that have not yet been enacted. It is consequently impossible to be fully acquainted with all the considerations for and against the future execution of any given law. If the duty to obey the law involves one's advance consent to forgo any possible action based on unforeseen considerations, then acknowledging this duty means consenting to obey the law's directives while giving up the possibility of acting for moral reasons that may rule against this obedience.[12] Thus, this act of renunciation entraps the renouncer in a logical contradiction. How can he or she acknowledge a moral commitment to perform acts whose performance may be decisively outruled by moral reasons? If the duty to obey the law comprises such a commitment, then it should be rejected outright, on purely logical grounds.[13]

[12] The danger that such reasons will indeed apply may be partly counteracted within the framework of a Natural-Law construal of the concept of law, and within constitutional legal systems. In both these cases it is predictable that laws cannot have contents contradicting certain values or constitutional directives. However, as to constitutions, they do not form necessary components of legal systems. And as to Natural-Law construals of the concept of law, the discussion here assumes, as stated (pp. 5–6 above), a positivistic interpretation of the concept of law, according to which rules and norms need not necessarily pass through moral filters of any kind so as to be considered laws in the legal sense.

[13] A well-known example of what I have called autonomy-based anarchism may be found in Robert Paul Wolff, *In Defense of Anarchism* (New York: Harper, 1970). This is also the position of the British nineteenth-century Utilitarian, William Godwin (Godwin, *Enquiry Concerning Political Justice*, ed. I. Kramnick [Harmondsworth: Penguin, 1976]). This type of anarchism may also be ascribed to Thoreau. (See H. D. Thoreau, "Civil Disobedience," *Walden and Civil Disobedience*, ed. S. Paul [Boston: Houghton Mifflin Co., 1960].) It should be noted forthwith that this anarchism is not anarchism in either the popular or the journalistic sense of the term. In these senses, anarchism is chaos, disorder, a war of all against all. The serious political theories classified as anarchist ones do not see such a state of affairs as their ideal. As Pierre Prudhon, father of modern political anarchism, clarified, they strive for the existence of a social order that doesn't rely on the existence of authority. The forms of anarchism anchored in social and philosophical theories do not deny the value of security and order, but they believe that these are maintainable without a state, without a government, without a monopoly of power. Anarchism in this sense is a general term for a wide range of theories, the central aspects of some of which are diametrically opposed. Rightwing anarchists, for instance, support the state's abolition as they believe business corporations to be capable of supplying order and security along with the other services they provide, while leftwing anarchists support the abolition of concentrations of political power, as they believe it possible and desirable to maintain communal societies in which the quality

The prospect of an autonomy-based anarchism can be fended off in one of two ways. The first, briefly intimated above, denies the very possibility of a situation where future conditions and laws could generate reasons overriding those in favor of obeying the law.[14] The second program, on the other hand, denies the rigid conception of the duty to obey.

As regards the first strategy, when the justifications of the duty to obey are seen as deriving from unchallengeable values, an acceptance of this duty runs no risk of surrendering moral autonomy. The normative position that views this duty as grounded on incontestable values, logically entails that it will outweigh other moral considerations in any instance involving it. Consider the case of a person who sees the duty to obey as justified on the basis of society's security and order, and deems these values which no other can possibly override. Such a person is not relinquishing moral autonomy when he or she acknowledges this duty as a surrender of possible action arising from judgments of the laws' contents. According to her or his normative position no value can ever override those of society's security and order, and as he or she sees the duty to obey the law as serving these values, a law's contents can never generate considerations that supersede them, given a situation to which the law applies. In such a case then, a complete advance surrender of any action based on considerations deriving from the contents of the law is no different from any other surrender of action based on reasons that have been

of human relations is such that no monopoly is necessary for the maintenance of order and security. The former are motivated by a wish to encourage individualistic enterprise, and the latter by a wish to encourage communitarian societies. Thus, what justifies or explains the classification of many political theses as anarchism is not their support of disorder and total war, but rather their denial of the necessity of institutions, or principles considered by popular political thought to be necessary, or almost necessary, for the preservation of social order: the state, a legal order monopolizing power and accompanied by sanctions, political classes, etc. The anarchism that I'm referring to here is of this type. Its proponents do not wish for, and do not advise, disorder and chaos, but they deny the extremely popular view that there is a duty to obey the law, and the view that the acknowledgment of such a duty is both necessary for and central to the existence of social order and security. This anarchism is also philosophical anarchism in the sense that it is content to point out fundamental philosophical considerations outruling the very moral possibility of political authority or of a duty to obey the law. It doesn't entail conclusions as to the suitable form of social organization or the means for replacing the forms in which humanity is presently organized with anarchist ones – matters which are at the very heart of the rightwing and leftwing anarchisms of the nineteenth and twentieth centuries. On the various forms of anarchism see David Miller, *Anarchism* (London: Dent and Sons, 1984).

[14] On this matter see also the discussion of the law's supremacy as possessed of inherent value, section 6, below.

overridden by alternative ones. Such a surrender is rationally motivated. As such, it naturally poses no contradiction to moral autonomy. On the contrary, it constitutes a definitive and characteristic manifestation of such an autonomy. Autonomy-based anarchism will thus leave unimpressed a position that bases the duty to obey upon values it sees as incontestable, while adopting the rigid conception of this duty.

This, however, is not the program I shall present against the anarchism in question. I will try to refute the conceptual thesis according to which an acknowledgment of the duty to obey, by virtue of its very meaning, involves refraining from actions motivated by considerations which follow from the laws' contents. I shall make no attempt to confirm the normative thesis according to which the duty to obey is supported by values whose weight is so decisive as to rule out any possible challenge. My choice to refute the conceptual thesis is based on the following considerations: if indeed autonomy-based anarchism possesses any power of attraction whatsoever, if there is any point in addressing it as more than a merely negligible whim, this is only because the conceptual thesis has real and diverse roots in the concept of the duty to obey. On the other hand, the normative thesis lacks such roots in the value systems of most people. (Were the conceptual thesis obviously mistaken, the claims of autonomy-based anarchism would have nothing to oppose. Were the normative thesis obviously right, these claims would have no grounds.) Clearly, there is no philosophical interest in opposing anarchism through a confirmation of the normative thesis, a thesis almost completely lacking any attraction, to which almost none fall prey. Clearly, too, there is much philosophical interest in opposing it through a refutation of the conceptual thesis, a thesis with very real roots and mistakenly adopted by many.

In opposing autonomy-based anarchism through a refutation of the rigid view of the duty to obey, I am choosing a road already traveled by other authors. However, as I shall show shortly, they made only part of the journey, and limped to boot. They understood the duty to obey the law as a *prima facie* duty, i.e. a duty whose justifications require execution only when they are sounder than the moral reasons against the duty's performance. In adopting this conception, the authors in question thought to put an end to the view that the duty to obey the law entails a surrender of moral autonomy. They didn't, though, for two reasons. First, and less important, while the basic idea seminal to the concept of *prima facie* duty is a sound one, the explanations offered for this concept are not completely satisfactory. Second, and much more important, it is not only the duty component in the concept of the duty to obey the law which leads to an understanding of this duty as necessarily involving the absolute performance of the actions falling under it. This concept has at least four other components that would seem, on the face of it, to entail its rigid interpretation, either separately or jointly. Firstly, being a duty to obey the law, its acknowledgment involves a willingness to perform actions for the reason that others (the legislators) wish them performed. Secondly, it is a duty to obey the law in the sense of legal norm, and thus a duty to obey commands. Consequently, a willingness to perform the acts it requires must somehow involve necessity. Thirdly, it is a duty to obey the law in the sense of social institution, an institution perceived as ultimate and supreme. Fourth, as a duty to obey the law, it is a duty to obey commands the contents of which should be based on the best possible judgment of the matter to which they pertain.

My discussion will now deal with these four components of the duty-to-obey concept, as well as elaborating further upon the duty component itself. I shall attempt to show how the concept's rigid construal and its complementary pole, autonomy-based anarchism, grow out of these components. I shall then try to show that this is a case of growth run wild.

3. *BECAUSE* THE LAW SO COMMANDS

Acknowledging the duty to obey the law means acknowledging that there is reason for performing the acts it ordains merely because it so ordains.[15] This (by no coincidence) is one of the concept's more important aspects, one which is worthy of emphasis. Many of the acts ordained by the law are duties independently of the fact of their legal ordainment, or are required for reasons which would apply in any case. For example: most of us recognize a duty to refrain from fraud, theft and homicide. The law too prescribes this refrainment.

---

[15] See also: M. B. E. Smith, "Is There a *Prima Facie* Obligation to Obey the Law?" *Yale Law Journal* 82 (1973), 950, pp. 950–2; Raz, *The Authority of Law*, pp. 233–4; Philip Soper, "The Obligation to Obey the Law" in Ruth Gavison (ed.), *Issues in Contemporary Legal Philosophy – The Influence of H. L. A. Hart* (Oxford: Oxford University Press, 1987), pp. 128, 132.

However, acknowledgment of the duty to obey the law means acknowledging this refrainment as a duty not merely because it is one anyway. It means acknowledging that the very fact of its ordainment by law binds it with a reason which makes it mandatory, a reason that wouldn't have had this effect had the refrainment not been so ordained.

The link between an act's ordainment by law and its emergence as a duty is a highly complex one. I shall treat some of its aspects elsewhere in my discussion.[16] In the present context, though, it is important to note how it leads to the misconception that the duty to obey involves an advance surrender, on the part of its acknowledgers, of actions based on their wills and evaluations. It does so jointly with another truth about obeying the law, a truth which follows from the meaning of the term law. Obeying the law means obeying something whose creation and contents don't depend on the wishes and discretion of the individual bound by duty to obey it, but depend, rather, on the wills and discretion of others: the legislators. This, in combination with the fact that the duty to obey means a duty to perform acts because the law so orders, leads some writers to identify this duty with a willingness on the part of its acknowledgers to subject themselves to the wills of others and relinquish their moral autonomy. "The autonomous man," Robert Paul Wolff tells us, after under-lining the aspect of obedience currently under discussion, "...is not subject to the will of another. He may do what another tells him, but not *because* he has been told to do it."[17] In other words, in doing something because someone else has told you to, you subject your will

---

[16] See below, chapter 2, section 4.

[17] See Wolff, *In Defense of Anarchism*, p. 14. As the text clarifies, this view of Wolff's is totally unacceptable. This is so on the condition that the "because" he uses when speaking of doing things because others say so denotes a reason rather than a cause. As shown in the text itself, the duty to obey the law implies a *justificational* link between the fact of an act being demanded by law and its becoming a duty, and such links of reason are expressed through the word "because." This word, however, is confusingly ambiguous. It has two senses, one having to do with reason or justification, and the other with cause. Beliefs in the existence of reasons are often used in causal explanations of behavior, whether or not these are good and sufficient reasons for the conduct caused by the belief. If Wolff's "because" denotes such a cause, a cause which is a mistaken belief in the existence of a reason, and not a good and sufficient reason, then he is correct. If someone else's word is the cause of my conduct when it shouldn't have given reason for this conduct, then I am not autonomous in this conduct. However, if this is what Wolff's argument implies it should clearly be rejected outright, as it begs the question quite grossly. It presupposes that the law's command cannot be the reason for performing what it prescribes, and this is precisely what Wolff sets out to prove and can thus not presuppose, not even implicitly.

to that of another and end your autonomous status. You necessarily and totally debar yourself from acting on considerations that stem from your manner of judging either others' wills or the conditions under which you should comply with them.

The futility of this last thesis is easily demonstrated by the willingness most of us show to comply with the requests of others, at least sometimes with the requests of some others, and the clear desirability of possessing such a willingness. This is so obvious that it makes any explanation rather embarrassing. I offer one nonetheless, as its details prepare the ground for my subsequent discussions of the other claims supporting the rigid conception of the duty to obey, claims which, on the face of it at least, seem much more convincing.

Our willingness to perform acts because others desire it, implicit in both our willingness to comply with others' requests and our willingness to obey the law, endows others with two types of power. It endows them with the power to create reasons for certain actions (or at least to create situations so as to make certain reasons apply to certain actions). It also empowers them to determine the acts whose performance these reasons require. When someone, a certain amount of whose requests I'm more or less willing to fulfill, asks something of me, his or her will alone (expressed through the request) prompts the reasons for fulfilling requests in general, and his or her requests in particular, to apply to the requested act, and become a reason for its performance. Clearly, though, my willingness to leave these powers at his or her disposal doesn't involve a willingness on my part to suspend judgment of the use he or she makes of them. Nor does it involve a willingness on my part to abstain totally from any action based on such judgments of mine.

Someone may exploit my willingness to comply with his or her requests too frequently or make especially burdensome requests too often. He or she may, intentionally or unintentionally, request something the performance of which will injure him or her or myself. In such cases I will weigh all of this against the considerations favoring the act's performance due to the mere fact of its having been requested. The outcome will form my answer to the question whether or not to perform the requested deed. A decision to perform the requested act won't imply a total, advance surrender, on my part, of any possibility of acting on reasons that may arise from the act's contents or the circumstances of its performance. If I decide to perform it this will be because the reasons against its performance were considered within the specific context, and were finally outweighed by the converse reasons arising from the very fact of its being requested.

In other words, a willingness to act because others wish and request it doesn't mean an advance consent to refrain, absolutely, from action due to reasons following from the contents of these wishes or from the circumstances of their application. There is no implication that a request's execution doesn't depend (among other things) on the timing of this request, the frequency and substance of the requesters' wishes, the specific nature of these requesters, etc. The fact that such a willingness must accompany any acknowledgment of the duty to obey, accordingly doesn't imply that this duty involves, of necessity, an absolute advance abstention from disobeying the law for reasons arising from its contents and conditions of application. Moreover, this fact most certainly doesn't imply that the duty to obey the law necessarily involves a subjection of one's will and a surrender of moral autonomy.[18] Such a surrender would mean the surrender of action based upon one's independent and overall judgment. As shown above, a willingness to perform actions for the reason that others wish it involves no relinquishment of action based on either independent or overall judgment.

---

[18] Wolff's claims imply that a subjection of the will and a surrender of moral autonomy are one and the same. This, however, is a mistake. Two conditions must be met in order that you may be said to be subjecting your will to a second party's, in performing a given action. 1. It must be the case that you do not want to perform this action. 2. You must be of the opinion that the second party shouldn't desire (or demand) you to perform this action. That the first condition is not sufficient may be seen from the multitude of situations where we perform actions requested by others though they are inconvenient. We do not view ourselves as subjecting our wills in every case of this type. For instance, we only consider helping friends move to be a subjection of our will to theirs when they make requests which they shouldn't have and we comply, in the belief that we should. We only see ourselves as subjecting our will to our commander's when his commands are such that they shouldn't be given, and we nonetheless comply with them for similar reasons. In such subjections of will, however, we are not surrendering our autonomy. Some requests, though they shouldn't have been made in the first place, should be fulfilled once they have been made. For instance, a friend who has helped us a great deal asks us to deliver 30 kilograms of (non-urgent) baggage on our next flight overseas, when the weight limit is 20 kilograms and we have baggage of our own. This request should not have been made, perhaps, but once it has, there may be situations in which it should be fulfilled. The person fulfilling it subjects his or her will, but doesn't surrender his or her moral autonomy. A surrender of moral autonomy only exists where a person acts against his or her overall judgment as to what he or she should do. You are only surrendering your moral autonomy when you view the wishes with which you comply not only as wishes which should not have been (or must not be) made, but also as wishes which should not be fulfilled. Autonomous man may, and sometimes should, subject his will to that of others.

There are, however, three additional points each of which, when it is considered in the context of the duty to obey the law and combined with the aspects of obedience presently under discussion, nonetheless seems to entail the rigid conception of the duty to obey, and through it an autonomy-based anarchism. The first of these is the fact that the context in question, as opposed to that of fulfilling requests, has to do with a *duty*.

4. A *DUTY* TO OBEY

We habitually consider acts that we are duty-bound to perform to be identical with acts which must be performed. In the absence of such an identification, we would be at a loss to explain the difference between acts that constitute duties (keeping promises, telling the truth, not killing), and acts that are merely considered desirable (aiding the elderly, nursing the sick, etc.). This is a card that will undoubtedly be played by someone attempting to show that the duty to obey entails a surrender of moral autonomy, after having failed to do so on the grounds of our willingness to perform acts just because others want them performed. Such a contender will claim that acknowledging the duty to obey the law, unlike one's willingness to comply with requests, involves more than presenting others with the power of creating reasons for action (or creating situations to which such reasons will apply). As what is involved here is mandatory performance, such acknowledgment gives them power to create absolute reasons for actions, thus totally appropriating the acknowledger's power to act upon his or her own judgment.

I have already cited the present component of the duty to obey as the one focused upon by contenders against anarchism. They reject the claim that acknowledging the duty to obey necessarily entails a surrender of autonomy, pointing out the possibility of its construal as a *prima facie* duty, which does not necessarily involve performance of the actions falling under it.[19]

---

[19] For instance: J. H. Reiman, *In Defense of Political Philosophy* (New York: Harper, 1972), pp. 55–6. The concept of a *prima facie* duty was brought to the center of philosophical debate by the British philosopher, W. D. Ross, in the second chapter of his book, *The Right and the Good* (Oxford, 1930). At times Ross explains it as a non-real duty. At other times he talks about it as a "tendency to be one's duty," and on yet other occasions it is explained as a non-absolute duty. Ross' explanations touch upon aspects which are central to the functioning of generic duties in moral thinking and psychology. However, they are notorious for their confusions and vagueness and certainly need not be analyzed in detail for the purposes of the present argument. See discussions of them in P. F. Strawson, "Ethical Intuitionism," *Philosophy* 24 (1949), 23; J. R. Searle, '*Prima Facie* Obligations" in Joseph Raz (ed.),

Those who speak of *prima facie* duties, are in fact referring to generic duties, in an attempt to say that the peremptory force of these is not final or decisive, as opposed to the peremptory force of judgments expressing final conclusions of particular practical deliberations. Judgments expressing such conclusions dictate, decisively, what is to be done in the situations to which they apply, as they are products of a balance of all the considerations relevant to the given situations.[20] We tend to confuse the peremptory force of such judgments with that of generic duties, as the same vocabulary, words such as "must," "has to," "ought," is used to express both.[21] The term *prima facie* duty is thus used in order to stress that what is involved is not a "must" expressing the final outcome of a practical, concrete deliberation, but rather an abstract, generic duty, whose peremptory force is not absolute.

What then, is this peremptory force? The *prima facie* duty to keep promises, says Gilbert Harman, means that "if you have promised to do something, that gives you moral reason to do what you have promised to do."[22] John Searle takes a similar position: *prima facie* duties or generic duties are reasons for action, not necessarily totally decisive reasons.[23] They are reasons that can sometimes be over-ridden. This understanding of generic duties clarifies the possibility of adhering to them while at the same time being of the opinion that they should not be carried out (and indeed not carrying them out in practice) without encountering a contradiction. Thus, it certainly makes place for the possibility of adhering to the duty to obey the law without making the slightest concession as to one's independent judgment and moral autonomy. But it achieves this at the price of overlooking one of the main points due to which duties are so complex from a conceptual point of view. It ignores the need to

Practical Reasoning (Oxford: Oxford University Press, 1978); H. J. McCloskey, "Ross and the Concept of *Prima Facie* Duty," *Australian Journal of Philosophy* 41 (1963), 336.

[20] For example, we may consider the question whether the terminal illness of a close relative is reason enough to miss work. After taking account of various factors which we deem relevant (the urgency of the work awaiting us, the possibility of its completion by someone else, the possibility that another relative might tend the sick-bed, etc.) we reach the conclusion that the reasons for tending the sickbed are infinitely stronger than those in favor of going to work and that, therefore, we ought to stay with him, that we have a duty to do so.

[21] See also Bernard Williams, "Practical Necessity" in Williams, *Moral Luck* (Cambridge: Cambridge University Press, 1981), p. 124; Simmons, *Moral Principles and Political Obligations*, pp. 7–11.

[22] Gilbert Harman, "Reasons" in Raz (ed.), *Practical Reasoning*, p. 114.

[23] Searle, "*Prima Facie* Obligations."

distinguish them from actions which are morally desirable only. If duties are actions for whose performance there are moral reasons, *simpliciter*, what is it that distinguishes them from actions which are just morally desirable?

This question would seem to thrust us back to the thesis from which we began, the basis ventured by those who see the duty to obey the law as entailing a surrender of autonomy. We seem to be back at the view that generic duties indicate the existence of final and absolute reasons for performing the actions falling under such duties, reasons entailing the mandatory performance of these actions.

But are there any ways of avoiding such a setback? It seems there are. One of these, which I see as more successful than the others,[24] is understanding generic duties as having to do with limited practical musts. They can be understood as act-types whose performance is a must as long as the reasons against it are of certain types, of personal convenience, for instance, or other a-moral reasons. Their performance will not be a must, however, when the reasons against it are of other types, when they are values such as freedom and equality, for example. In other words, generic duties denote act-types that are supported by reasons which enjoy absolute precedence, in the context of these act-types, not to every possible reason for action but to certain reasons only.[25] For example, the duty to refrain from homicide

---

[24] McCloskey, *Meta-Ethics and Normative Ethics*, suggests that *prima facie* duties be understood as follows: "To be *prima facie* obliged to do A, is for there to be powerful moral reasons for doing A which constrains me to do A. However, they need not be knockdown reasons, and they may be reasons which other moral reasons may override" (p. 243). This definition grantedly points out a difference between duties and mere reasons, but it too is unsatisfactory. It provides no sufficient or necessary conditions for being a duty. There are actions supported by weighty moral reasons which we nonetheless do not see as duties: for example, acts of heroism in the battle field. Also, there are actions supported by trivial reasons which we still consider to be duties – trivial promises, for instance.

Another suggestion for understanding duties is the one that may be derived from Raz's view of mandatory rules. According to him, such rules have two functions in the world of our moral thinking. First, they function as second-order reasons, reasons for not acting on other reasons. As such they exclude specific types of reasons for action from the balance of reasons pertaining to the action which is the subject of the duty. In this capacity Raz calls them "exclusionary reasons." Second, they function as ordinary, first-order reasons, competing with all the other reasons which they haven't excluded, through a comparison of respective weights. Raz's theory of mandatory rules is much more adequate than any of the rest so far mentioned. However, it has many drawbacks the analysis of which is not relevant for the purposes of the present argument. I have criticized his understanding of mandatory rules in my "Mandatory Rules and Exclusionary Reasons," *Philosophia* 15 (1985–6), 373.

[25] Some may claim that any action at all can enjoy the support of a reason with precedence over other reasons, and that duties as characterized by the proposed conception are accordingly indistinguishable from other actions. It would seem, however, that this claim misses the point of the proposal. When performing an action for a reason which overrides

has absolute precedence over certain kinds of reasons, such as those of personal convenience or financial interests, but not over every possible reason, cases in point being the values of liberty and equality. When the actual avoidance of killing will cause harm to these latter, the decision whether or not to kill will depend on the intensity of the damage caused these values under the circumstances of the given killing. So too, as regards the duty to obey the law. It has absolute precedence over some reasons for action only, such as personal convenience, not over all possible reasons, including those of liberty and justice. Thus, when a specific instance of obedience will damage the latter values, the decision whether or not to obey will depend on the intensity of the damage caused these values under the circumstances of the given instance.

This understanding of generic duties clarifies their especial peremptory aspect, distinguishing them from merely desirable actions, an aspect missed by the understanding offered by Harman and Searle. By the same token, it also clarifies the possibility of adhering to duties without totally surrendering the option of considering their non-performance, and at times refraining from this performance, in the actual circumstances to which they apply. The last possibility exists because a conflict between a duty and reasons (or duties) relative to which it does not enjoy absolute precedence is solved in the way in which practical conflicts are usually solved: by weighing the comparative intensities of the conflicting considerations.

In short, I have suggested a conception of generic duties at large and the duty to obey in particular as practical musts of limited absoluteness. On such a view, the question whether willingness to obey the law involves an advance surrender of the option of disobeying for reasons based on the law's substance or circumstances of application cannot be answered with reference to the fact that the willingness in question is a willingness to obey out of duty. The decision depends on answers to questions on the scope of the reasons relative to which this duty has absolute precedence. The question

---

another, we are not necessarily committed to the view that this reason will always do so, with regard to the action presently supported by it and the reasons presently overridden by it. If I decide to attend a concert instead of visiting a friend, my decision doesn't acknowledge an absolute preference on my part as the reason for my present decision on the concert, over the present reason for visiting my friend. This is not the case when I decide not to rob a bank, though such an action could easily improve my financial condition. I conceive of my reason for not robbing the bank as one which enjoys absolute precedence over considerations of my financial well-being.

whether reasons pertaining to the law's substance and its circumstances of application, as such, do or do not fall within this scope,
is a normative rather than conceptual one. It cannot be contended
that by virtue of the duty component of the duty to obey,
acknowledgment of this duty means a surrender of the option to
refrain from obeying, for reasons pertaining to the law's contents.

Two aspects of the concept of the duty to obey have been discussed
so far, then. First: obeying the law means performing acts because
others desire it. Second: obeying the law is a duty. Whether taken
together or separately, these fundamental truths do not serve to show
that an acknowledgment of the duty to obey the law involves a total
advance surrender of the option to disobey for reasons arising from
the law's substance or circumstances of application. The fact that
obeying the law is a duty gives no grounds for the apprehension that
this duty's acknowledgment involves an advance sacrifice of the
option to act on unanticipated reasons. Thus it does not entail a
surrender of moral autonomy. However, this conclusion may still
follow from yet another truth about the duty to obey the law, that
according to which it is a duty to obey *commands*.

5. LAWS AS COMMANDS

The duty to obey the law is a duty to obey commands. This truth
stems from the concept of law and not from those of obedience or
duty. What the term "law" denotes, in one of its senses, is the legal
norm, and the legal norms involved in the context of the duty to obey
the law are commands.[26] A willingness to obey commands is
commonly thought to imply the addressee's willingness to submit to
the commander all final decisions on practical matters pertaining to
the command. A willingness to obey commands is thus thought to
imply a complete surrender, on the part of their acknowledgers, of
the option to disobey them for reasons arising from their substance.
In other words, it means a surrender of moral autonomy. "Taking

---

[26] Theorists of law differ as to whether all laws are commands. Austin and Kelsen answer in
the affirmative. Hart believes that some laws are norms rather than commands (see H. L.
A. Hart, *The Concept of Law* [Oxford: Oxford University Press, 1961], ch. 3). Raz holds that
not only is it the case that not all laws are commands, not all laws are norms either (see
Joseph Raz, *The Concept of a Legal System* [Oxford: Oxford University Press, 1970], ch. 7).
The controversy on this issue, however, is based on differences in theoretical considerations
as to the functions of descriptive and analytical jurisprudence, and has no bearing upon our
subject.

responsibility for one's own actions," says Wolff, "means making the final decisions about what one should do. For the autonomous man there is no such thing as a command."[27]

The construal of commands as absolute and final and the analogous interpretation of duties share a single point of origin. Both need to be distinguished from their close relatives. What is needed, in the case of acts that are considered duties is, as we have already seen, an explanation of how they differ from acts that are merely considered desirable. What is needed in the case of commands is an explanation of how they differ from requests.[28] Both commands and requests are speech acts through which their performers intend to provide their addressees with reasons for action. If this is the whole story though, what, if any, is the difference between the two? Here too, as with the attempt to distinguish desirable acts from acts that count as duties, many are quick to suggest finality as the basis of the distinction. Commands are said to involve an intent to create final reasons for action, while requests are ascribed the intent of creating reasons which the receiver is entitled to consider and reject. Acknowledging requests accordingly doesn't involve a total surrender of their possible rejection for reasons following from their contents. Acknowledging commands turns out, under Wolff's analysis, to involve, necessarily, at least such a surrender.

The theory of commands as final reasons is superfluous and unsatisfactory for just the same reasons that make the theory of duties as final reasons superfluous and unsatisfactory. I will accordingly be brief on the present point. The difference between commands and requests may be explained in the same terms used above to explain the difference between general duties and generally desirable acts. It is possible and advisable to conceive of the absoluteness of duties as a limited one. It is equally possible and advisable to conceive of commands' absoluteness in a like manner. Commands may be disobeyed, but only for specific kinds of reasons, not for all possible reasons. Requests can and should be conceived of as reasons for performing the acts they specify, reasons which don't necessarily

---

[27] Wolff, *In Defense of Anarchism*, p. 15.
[28] In section 3 I also employed a comparison to requests. It should, perhaps, be emphasized that their role in the former comparison differs from their present role. There, they were used to reject the thesis that a willingness to perform actions because others wish it means a surrender of autonomy. I am using them here to corroborate the thesis that a willingness to obey commands involves a surrender of autonomy, a thesis which I shall disprove further along.

override any other, specific types of reasons. Requests may be rejected for any reason at all. This will suffice to explain the difference between requests and commands. There is no need to view commands as absolute and final reasons for the acts they stipulate. Even commands contradict each other on occasion, which makes the modest conception of their decisiveness all the more advantageous. They should be viewed as supplying absolute reasons for action, enjoying absolute precedence only to specific types of other reasons, and not to all possible reasons. What I am saying, then, is that the necessity associated with commands can be understood in the same manner as the necessity associated with duties. Both can be read as a limited absoluteness. This means that a willingness to acknowledge and obey them does not contradict the possibility of disobeying them for reasons pertaining to their substance or their circumstances of application.

To sum up, this section has examined the fact that a recognition of the duty to obey the law constitutes an acknowledgment of the duty to obey commands. Despite (misleading) first impressions, this fact does not imply that the duty in question involves a willingness to surrender, totally and in advance, the option of disobedience for reasons following from the law's contents or circumstances of application. Here too then, the duty to obey is found innocent of the charge of entailing a surrender of moral autonomy. However, there is still one serious conceptual claim, more serious perhaps than any that I have discussed so far, supporting the thesis that the duty to obey must involve such a surrender. This claim has to do with the supremacy and finality that most of us associate, and as we shall see with no mean degree of justice, with the law in the sense of social institution.

6. THE SUPREMACY OF LAW

The duty to obey the law is a duty to obey the orders of a certain social institution, the legal system of a community. Among the characteristics we commonly associate with the law in this sense are supremacy and finality. This is only a few steps from autonomy-based anarchism as it may seem to entail that each and every legal injunction is supreme and final. This, however, is a false impression, as we shall see when we are clearer about our association of law with supremacy and finality.

Under one interpretation, the law's supremacy is a factual–

conceptual matter. Just as an object cannot count as a chair if it isn't meant for sitting, so this thesis runs, and just as a person cannot count as a robber if he never employs either threats or force to demand others' property, a social institution cannot count as the community's legal system if it fails to claim supremacy and succeed in realizing this claim. It is possible and correct to understand the supremacy of the law in this way. This is so simply because it is a pre-analytic factual datum about the phenomenon forming the central interest of jurisprudence and because the question of the duty to obey concerns obedience to institutions of which this thesis is true.[29] In referring to the law and the duty to obey it, what we have in mind is the supreme normative system practiced within a community.[30] Modern human communities make use of many sorts of normative systems. This very differentiation is one of the principal driving forces behind modern theorizing about the law, and its attempts to distinguish, systematically, the features of the law which set it apart from other normative systems utilized by human communities (e.g. ideal morality; positive morality; etiquette; the normative system of

[29] It is easy to see that this claim is correct when we remind ourselves of our manner of expression upon discovering that what purports to be the community's legal system fails to claim supremacy and tacitly accepts the normative decisions of other institutions opposing its own rules. In Israel such states of affairs are sometimes approached in the disputes between the secular legal authorities and the Rabbinate along with the religious tribunals. When the latter demand supremacy and the former remain silent, we indeed begin to wonder just who represents the law here.

[30] The anarchism discussed in this chapter is not aimed against, or in any way dependent upon, the means employed by the community's supreme normative system to achieve this supremacy. (See also Wolff, *In Defense of Anarchism*, p. 3.) One should thus be cautious and avoid conclusions drawn from the disproval of this form of anarchism, as to the truth of other, no less important forms of anarchism, and especially that attacking the modern mass state that attains order and stability not only through the existence of a supreme normative system within its framework, but also by monopolizing the physical power within the community, attaching it to this normative system, and creating a differentiation of political offices. (See Michael Taylor, *Community, Anarchy and Liberty* [Cambridge: Cambridge University Press, 1982].) Although supreme normative systems in modern communities attain their supremacy through a monopoly of the physical power within the community and through sanctions, it would be incautious to see this as evidence that a monopoly of physical power and the use of sanctions are essentially definitive of law in general, as many believe. (This includes Austin, Kelsen and Hart; Raz disagrees very convincingly – see Joseph Raz, *Practical Reason and Norms* [London: Hutchinson, 1975], pp. 154–62.) They are most certainly not important, definitive characteristics of the law, for purposes of the subject of the present discussion. One should furthermore cautiously avoid understanding the fact that the supreme normative systems in modern communities usually exist within national communities as grounds for the conclusion that the national state is an essential, definitive characteristic of the law (as Kelsen would seem to believe; see Hans Kelsen, *General Theory of Law and State* [New York: Russel and Russel, 1961], pp. 182–3). It is most certainly not an essential, definitive characteristic of the law for purposes of the subject of the present discussion.

voluntary associations, etc.). The law's claim for supremacy appears in contemporary theories of law as an insight, an aspect which throws light on the difference between law and other normative systems such as those of universities, clubs and corporations.[31] Identifying the law with supremacy is also correct in the case of the law of primitive societies,[32] but there this identification cannot be presented as an insight, as it is probable that only one normative system was in force within such communities, hence leaving nothing from which to distinguish this system, and no rivals relative to which it could have claimed supremacy. The association of law with supremacy is thus a central, pre-theoretical, factual feature of the phenomenon known as law and constituting the central subject of jurisprudence, the phenomenon to which the question of the duty to obey pertains. In acknowledging the duty to obey the law, one is acknowledging a duty to obey the orders of an institution which demands supremacy for its orders and succeeds in enforcing this demand.[33] This is so for the simple reason that this is the type of system under discussion.

However, it doesn't follow from the above that *ipso facto* one has acknowledged the justifiability of this demand or the supremacy of the duty in question. No more than a person's actual readiness to do whatever his friend asks follows from his readiness to respond to this friend's requests and the fact that the friend has asked that all his requests be granted. The question whether or not the law's demand for supremacy is indeed justified is a substantive moral question. It is a meta-legal question, or even a meta-jurisprudential question. Any attempt to answer it within the law will only cause the question to regress to the answer which the law provides, and so on *ad infinitum*.

---

[31] See Raz, *Practical Reason and Norms*, pp. 149–52. Pointing out the existence of a claim to supremacy and its realization is not the only way of distinguishing between the normative systems cited in the text as similar in structure to the legal system. See, for instance, the manner in which Sartorious views Hart's distinction between them: Rolf Sartorious, "Hart's Concept of Law" in R. S. Summers (ed.), *More Essays in Legal Philosophy* (Oxford: Oxford University Press, 1971), p. 131, section 4. On the political system as characterized by a claim to supremacy, see also T. Machan, "Individualism and the Problem of Political Authority," *Monist* 66 (1983), 500, p. 513.

[32] Again, some theorists, such as Hart, will view the supreme normative system of primitive communities as a borderline case of law. See Hart, *The Concept of Law*, pp. 89–96. But his correct observations are irrelevant for purposes of our discussion.

[33] The answer to the question, what are the criteria for success in this matter, is a complex one. Is it enough for the majority to act in accordance with the system's commands? Should it act thus because the system so commands it? Is it enough that the combination of those who act on the system's commands and those whom the system succeeds in punishing for their disobedience forms the majority of those whom the system sees as its subjects? See Raz, *The Concept of a Legal System*, ch. 11.

The question of whether there is a moral duty to obey the law cannot be answered by a legal enactment for the original question will immediately be applied to this legal enactment itself. By the same token, the question of whether the moral duty to obey the law constitutes a supreme moral duty is one that cannot be solved by pointing to the jurisprudential and political truth that the law in fact claims supremacy. This truth supplies no answer as it, in turn, is subject to the question whether the claim the law makes is morally justified.

However, our association of law with supremacy *could* be understood as consisting not only of a descriptive–conceptual thesis. It could also be understood as a normative thesis. One normative construal of the law's claim to supremacy ascribes supreme intrinsic value to the law. Its prescriptions could be considered constitutive of the moral worth of actions, or thought to express the real will of their subjects, while any desires of the subjects found incompatible with the law would be classified as false, whether they were motivated by misgivings concerning the contents of the law or independently. Such a position would clearly give reason to acknowledge the validity of the law's claim to supremacy. Were this indeed the basis for the law's claim to supremacy, then acknowledging this claim would certainly entail an absolute surrender of the option to act against it for reasons arising from its content. The very possibility that any such reasons could direct one to disobey the law would be perceived in this case as either unthinkable or mistaken. Luckily (for my argument) no one seriously holds such a view of the value of law.[34] It is possible to ascribe a notion of this kind to Rousseau and Hegel, as regards laws originating in the mystic entities of the General Will or the State (in its specific Hegelian sense, namely, as an ethical and metaphysical absolute). But neither Rousseau nor Hegel entertained these thoughts with regard to laws in general. In the case of Rousseau they refer to the laws of direct democracies, and Hegel entertains them only with regard to the laws of states in the specific sense of this term within his metaphysics and his political theory. It seems, therefore, that autonomy-based anarchism cannot gain much support from the present conception of the supremacy of law.

[34] Were the present stance correct, then the moral duty to obey the law would acquire a meaning different from that generally possessed by moral duties. If the law institutes the moral value of actions, then asking whether we have a moral duty to obey it is like asking whether we have a duty to be moral. This question is of an entirely different dimension than that of questions as to the existence of particular moral duties.

The thesis of the law's supremacy could be construed as a normative one in another, different sense. It could be argued that the law is *right* in claiming supremacy on instrumental grounds, rather than grounds of intrinsic value. Demanding supremacy (with success) is, according to this view, a necessary requirement for the law if it is to perform its central social role as the institution determining and/or enforcing the desirable behavior of and within society. An instrumental justification of this kind seems to underlie the political theories of Hobbes and Locke. The ability of the law to function as the keeper of social order, stability and certainty, is founded upon its subjects' expectation that its directives, rather than remaining mere words, will be realized in practice. In anticipation of this realization, they base plans for their behavior on the law's directives. The law's failure to claim supremacy and/or to realize it would undermine its subjects' expectation that its directives be realized, rather than those of other organizations or bodies. This would weaken their reliance upon the law's directives, and its ability to determine and/or enforce desirable behavior would either decline or disappear altogether. The law's claim to supremacy and its ability to realize it are therefore central means through which it is able to realize its principal social function.

However, acknowledging the law's claim to supremacy under this justification doesn't imply readiness to carry out its directives regardless of their contents. Moreover, someone who acknowledges the duty to obey so as to support the law's role as a preserver of social order and stability may consider its demand for supremacy, and its success in realizing this demand, necessary conditions for such an acknowledgment. Nonetheless, even this does not mean that such a person intends to perform the law's directives under any circumstances. The situation here is similar to some in which we justifiably expect others to have and express certain desires or demands so that our wish to perform their exact opposite will be complete. Consider the case of wanting to help someone. Sometimes, in order that this desire of ours be complete, we can justifiably expect refusal of our help. This expectation is not necessarily justified because the person's refusal itself is justified, but rather because the desire he or she is expressing indicates that our help hasn't been taken for granted and thus that he or she deserves to be helped.[35] Or consider competitive

---

[35] Even more common are situations in which we wish others to make demands so that we will want to do the opposite, without it being morally justified to wish this. Without their logical

games. We expect our rivals in such games to harbor a serious desire to win, and possess a serious ability to carry out this desire. Otherwise the game would be pointless. But this does not mean that we want them to win, or that we believe it justified that they win every actual game. These cases are even more extreme than the one we are dealing with, namely, the instrumental justification of the law's claim to supremacy. They refer to situations where we consider it proper that the existence of others' desires form a condition for our justified performance of the opposite. The instrumental justification of the law's claim to supremacy is, on the other hand, a case in which the existence of a demand *may* form a precondition for our willingness to conform only in part to this demand (to acknowledge obedience to the law as a duty, i.e. to recognize its absoluteness relative to certain kinds of reasons for action). In short, just as competitive games are pointless when our opponents do not and cannot attempt to win, acknowledging the duty to obey the law is pointless when the law doesn't or can't claim supremacy. And yet, just as the first case of pointlessness doesn't mean that we are ready to give in to our opponent, neither does the second case entail our acknowledgment of the law's supremacy. In other words, when taken as an instrumental thesis, the thesis that the law is justified in claiming supremacy does not entail that the duty to obey the law implies a complete surrender of the option of breaking laws for reasons arising from their substance. It thus does not entail a surrender of moral autonomy, and autonomy-based anarchism is again foiled.

However, a serious difficulty may still be encountered here. How can an acknowledgment of the justness of the law's claim to finality be expressed in practice, if it is an acknowledgment that falls short of total practical identification with this finality? If you acknowledge the duty to obey the law and the justness of its claim to finality without acknowledging the finality of its claims, how can you express these acknowledgments of yours in practice? If you can find no way to do so, you are destined to seem inconsistent in deed and word.

In attempting to solve this quandary, it is first worth noting that if there is indeed a problem here, it doesn't arise from a contradiction between two opinions one of which must thus be given up. Second, what we are dealing with here is only the semblance of a

---

possibility, one of the channels of mundane evil could not exist. In the text, I preferred an example which not only illustrates the logical possibility of such states, but also their moral possibility.

contradiction. What one is destined to here, if anything, is seeming, not being, inconsistent in deed and word. If acknowledging the necessity of the law's claim to finality truly doesn't entail a complete surrender of the option of disobeying, then such disobedience may express a repudiation of the law's *actual* finality in view of all relevant considerations, and not a repudiation of the necessity of its *claim* to finality. The question as to what a given act of disobedience expresses must be answered in terms of the agent's reasons for this particular act. These reasons can be learned by asking the disobeyer. When it turns out that they have to do with the contents of the law or its circumstances of application, then there need not be any contradiction between the fact of disobedience and the position according to which the law is justified in claiming finality. There is no contradiction here between word and deed. Of course, the possibilities of deceit are extensive here, just as they are in all cases where intent is of interest. Deceit, however, makes the problem one of inconsistency of thought and word, not inconsistency of word and deed, a different problem entirely.

Moreover, you are not only not destined to be inconsistent in word and deed, you are also not destined to seem so. Even when you break the law your acknowledgment that its claim to finality is called for need not be relegated to the spheres of thought and speech alone. It may still be expressed at additional levels, those of your moral sentiments and, what is most important, your actions. The most heroic way of expressing your commitment to the justness of the law's claim to finality is to submit yourself to its penalty, openly and of your own free will, even as you disobey it. Less heroic ways of showing this commitment are criticizing the law's agents for failing to do what is necessary for the manifestation of the law's claim to finality and supremacy, though you yourself are attempting to dodge its penalty. If, after disobeying, you are punished without having wished it (and without, after consideration, having recognized the justness of such wishes) you will nonetheless be understanding and forgiving towards the law for punishing you. The necessity of its claim to finality provides the law with an excuse, if not with a justification, for such punishment. If the law fails to penalize you, you can, along with your relief and satisfaction, feel sorrow on its behalf.[36] In other words, your

---

[36] The question, which is the way in which it is justified to express your recognition of the necessity of the law's claim to supremacy – by heroically submitting yourself to punishment,

acknowledgment of the instrumental justification for the claim to finality may be expressed through acts as well as feelings, even if you do not perform whatever the law demands under any circumstances, even if you don't give up, completely and in advance, any possibility of disobeying for reasons following from the law's contents or circumstances of application.[37]

In his recently published book, Kent Greenawalt offers a somewhat different presentation and solution of the problem posed by the law's claim to supremacy.[38] Greenawalt sees this claim as problematic, not because it conflicts with moral autonomy, but because it seems to contradict what we all know from experience: that most people do not perceive the law as the supreme arbitrator on their practical matters. He reconciles this contradiction through a distinction between two conceptions of the claim to supremacy. According to the first, strong conception, the law, in claiming finality, seriously intends to instruct people what to do. According to the second, the law's claim to supremacy is limited to the realm of law. In other words, the law is like a set of rules for the management of a competition. These rules tell the competitors the outcome of their behavior as regards the competition. They don't tell them what to do in view of all possible considerations. For instance, failure to show up for a game counts as a loss by these rules, and may even involve a fine, but the rules don't seriously intend for a competitor to favor participation over tending to a sick family member.

According to Greenawalt, there is no need to assign the law's claim to supremacy the strong interpretation. Though many sense its correctness as regards serious crimes, Greenawalt contends that this is limited to such directives only and follows from an identification with their contents. The correctness of the strong conception of the law's claim to finality, in the context of serious criminal injunctions, should not lead to the conclusion that this finality is a feature of the rest of the law's directives as well.

---

by accepting it with resignation but without submission, or by attempting either to dodge it or forgive it should the former attempt fail – depends upon the circumstances of the disobedience and upon its justifications. For more on surrender to punishment see the fourth chapter, below, and: Rawls, *A Theory of Justice*, p. 366 and note 22; Kent Greenawalt, *Conflicts of Law and Morality* (Oxford: Oxford University Press, 1987), pp. 238–40; F. Olsen, "Socrates on Legal Obligation: Legitimation Theory and Civil Disobedience," *Georgia Law Review* 18 (1984), 929, p. 960.

[37] This theory must not be confused with the theory that the duty to obey the law is in fact merely the duty to take one's punishment.

[38] Greenawalt, *Conflicts of Law and Morality*, pp. 18–21.

As I see it, there are indeed legal areas in which the law's claim to supremacy may be understood in its weak sense. This is true, chiefly, of the area of civil law. It also seems correct that there are areas in which our identification with the law's substance serves to explain why the supremacy claim is understood in its strong sense. Such an explanation is true, as Greenawalt establishes, of the classical directives of criminal law; those prohibiting homicide, theft, rape, etc. However, Greenawalt's solution seems problematic when applied to the areas in which the importance of the duty to obey is highest; areas involving public controversy, be it moral or other (e.g. political questions or questions such as abortions or euthanasia). As regards such areas, it is a little difficult to understand the supremacy claim in its weak sense, or to explain people's identification with it in terms of their identification with the law's contents. When the law prohibits abortions, it would seem to do so subject to certain exceptions which it itself determines, all things considered. So too when it orders people to go to war. It intends to dictate the conduct of its subjects in a final manner, even if they do not identify with its contents, even if they object to its contents.

The law's claim for supremacy and the fact that many of its subjects fail to accept this claim at face value are not adequately reconciled, then, by Greenawalt's distinction and subsequent claims. It is not completely clear that the law's claim to finality may always be understood to lack any pretense to absolute decisiveness. My hope is that the present attempt to solve the contradiction will prove satisfactory. If I am right, then there is no need for Greenawalt's efforts to show that the law's supremacy claim should be construed as limited to its own realm. The question is not how the law understands its claim to finality, but how this claim should be understood by those that acknowledge the duty to obey it. The law's claim to supremacy may indeed be in conflict with a conception that holds the duty to obey it as less than supreme. This conflict, however, does not arise from a self-contradiction on the part of whoever acknowledges the duty to obey.

To sum up, acknowledging the duty to obey the law involves a willingness to obey an institution which we associate with supremacy and finality. This supremacy may be understood as a conceptual–descriptive thesis, namely, the thesis that the law is an institution which claims supremacy and is capable of realizing this claim. It may also be understood as a normative thesis, namely, the thesis that we should acknowledge the law's supremacy, as its claim to it is justified. As such, it can in turn be understood in two ways. The law's finality may be perceived as possessed of either intrinsic or instrumental value. It is only according to the intrinsic value version of the supremacy thesis that acknowledging the duty to obey entails a complete surrender of the option of disobedience for reasons based on the law's contents etc. This version, however, is unsound. A conception of the supremacy thesis either as a descriptive or a normative–instrumental one, doesn't entail the rigid conception of the duty to obey. It doesn't entail a loss of moral autonomy.

I now wish to discuss another one of the sources of the above misconception, a source that seemingly entails it on its own, independently of the various aspects of the duty to obey discussed so far. I'm referring to the attempt to apply our usual response to the orders of professional authorities such as doctors and lawyers to the context of the duty to obey. This attempt is yet another source of the rigid conception of this duty. The confusion stemming from this attempt is greater and more flagrant by far than that surrounding the previously discussed aspects. And yet, it is neither less prevalent nor less dangerous.

7. ACKNOWLEDGING AN AUTHORITY

The duty to obey the law is a duty to perform the acts specified by the instructions of legal authorities. Some see the impact of these instructions on our practical thought as analogous to that of the instructions of professional authorities such as doctors or lawyers. When following the instructions of such authorities, we surrender, according to this thesis, our independent discretion and judgment, or the possibility of acting on them. Acknowledging the duty to obey the law amounts to the same thing.[39] However, the argument proceeds, while there may be good reason to surrender our independent judgment and autonomy in matters whose evaluation is conducted by professional authorities, no such reasons apply to matters whose evaluation is conducted by legislators and other legal authorities. Acknowledging the duty to obey accordingly means an unjustified surrender of moral autonomy. Ergo, we must refuse to acknowledge this duty.[40]

---

[39] Wolff, *In Defense of Anarchism*, p. 15; H. L. A. Hart, *Essays on Bentham* (Oxford: Oxford University Press, 1982), p. 253.　　[40] Wolff, *In Defense of Anarchism*, p. 15.

This line of argument fails as it is simply not true that acknowledging authorities such as doctors or lawyers involves a complete surrender of independent judgment.[41] It also fails as it is not true that a surrender of action based on independent judgment necessarily constitutes a surrender of autonomy. However, the argument fails for other reasons as well. It fails because the analogy on which it is based is misleading. The rationale for obeying each type of authority is a different one. We follow the instructions of professional experts as we assume that they are based on evaluations the experts have made within their respective fields of expertise (doctors on medical matters, lawyers on legal matters, financial experts on stock market matters, etc.). If, in following the experts' instructions, we suspend our independent judgment of the matter dealt with by these instructions, or refrain from acting on such judgments, this is due to the fact that we assume their judgment on what we should do in the matter to be better than ours.[42] In the case of the legislature's instructions, there are no similar grounds for such an assumption. Even if there were, though, this assumption is by no means the essence of acknowledging the duty to obey.

In the case of professional authorities, unlike that of legal ones, the contents of their instructions may legitimately be presumed to be based on the best of judgment as regards the question: what should the recipients of these instructions do from the relevant practical point of view? For instance, it may legitimately be presumed that the contents of doctors' instructions are based on the best of their judgment as to what patients should do in the interests of their health. We may presume this on the basis of two prior assumptions. The first is that a professional authority itself has, at least in most cases, an interest in giving instructions that are based on the best of its professional judgment. Second, this (best of professional) judgment is accessible to the professional authority in question. This is just what makes it a professional authority. The best possible judgment of what a patient should do to cure his or her disease is accessible to a doctor. This is what makes him or her a doctor. Also, as mentioned above,

---

[41] See Flathman, *The Practice of Political Authority*, pp. 92–100; Raz, *The Morality of Freedom*, pp. 38–42.

[42] The fact that we are convinced of this is, itself, a result of our independent judgment. Thus, as stated at the beginning of this paragraph in the text, it is doubtful whether obedience to the instructions of professional authorities should be considered a surrender of autonomy at all. See also the discussions cited in the previous footnote.

the doctor's own interests supply a strong incentive to base his or her instructions to the patient on the best of judgment about what this patient should do for his health. Failing to do so will, at some point, cost him his livelihood. Even if there is room for these two presumptions in the context of legal authority, they are not sufficiently solid within this context. In this case, unlike that of professional authorities, it is doubtful whether the authority's self-interest requires it to exercise the best relevant judgment frequently enough to make it effective. As to the authority's access to the best possible relevant judgment: it may indeed have such access, but this is not necessarily true, as it is with professional authorities. In other words, Parliament's Financial Committee may include experts on economics and social justice, but this affords no solid grounds for presumptions regarding the economic effectivity and the social justness of the tax laws it proposes. Parliament's Financial Committee may also be peopled by some whose legislative work is motivated, entirely, by the economic good of the public as a whole. But not much store should be set by this possibility either.

Moreover, and this may be the main point, even if there were reason to perform the instructions of legal authorities due to well-grounded presumptions concerning their contents, their authority and our duty to obey them would still not lie, for the most part, in these reasons or this fact. In acknowledging this duty, we ac-knowledge the very fact that the law makes a requirement, as one that obligates us (*prima facie*) to perform the act specified by this requirement, even when the act is unjustified from other, relevant practical points of view. Our acknowledgment of the duty to obey the law is supposed to include an acknowledgment of the fact that the law requires payment of a certain percentage of our income as tax, as one which ties us to justifications for paying this amount of tax, even if it is unjustified in terms of economic efficiency and social justice. These justifications, which are discussed in detail in the next chapter, are related to the fact that failure to pay the tax as instructed by the legal authority, would usually make it difficult to ensure the existence of a public budget. They are also related to the fact that failing to carry out the authority's instructions would endanger its future functioning as a means of attaining goals of this type. The fact that a given act is commanded by law, links it with these justifications. It is they, and not the contents of the law, that are the whole point of acknowledging the duty to obey.

If there is indeed a duty to obey the law, then, it may be understood to be based on something other than the merits of the law's substance. Our reasons for obeying the instructions of professional authorities, on the other hand, are based exclusively on assumptions concerning their contents. The analogy between the two is accordingly precarious. It is therefore a mistake to conclude that obeying the law involves a surrender of discretion and judgment as regards the contents of its instructions and/or the circumstances of its application, in just the manner that obeying experts' instructions involves such a surrender.

It may be appropriate to note here that a single moral principle applies to both professional and legal authorities as regards the determination of their instructions. Both must base the contents of these instructions on the best of judgment regarding what their recipients should do in terms of the area to which the instructions apply, and not what they should do in terms of anything else. Doctors must base their instructions on their judgment of what will best serve their patients' health. Tax laws should be based on economic considerations and considerations of social justice. However, it is not because of this normative principle that we should treat such instructions as reasons for carrying out what they stipulate. As stated, in the context of professional authorities, the reasons for following their instructions are anchored in the contents of these instructions. This, however, does not follow from the *moral principle* according to which professional authorities must determine their instructions in accordance with the best possible relevant judgment. It follows, rather, from the existence of the well-grounded, *factual presumption* that they indeed do so. In the case of legal authority, on the other hand, the reasons for obedience derive from the need to preserve that authority as a social tool, not from the contents of its instructions.

A complex argument for a conception of practical authority, differing from the one suggested here, is presented in Professor Raz's book, *The Morality of Freedom*.[43] According to Raz, acknowledging practical authority (a category which can include any person whose sayings are authoritative reasons for action, including professional authorities) does, indeed, entail a willingness to refrain from action on the basis of objections to the contents of its instructions. This thesis

---

[43] Less detailed versions of this view may be found in his earlier books: *Practical Reason and Norms; The Authority of Law*. For critiques of the various aspects of the argument for this view see my "Mandatory Rules and Exclusionary Reasons," and also Michael Moore, "Authority, Law and Razian Reasons," *Southern California Law Review* 62 (1989), 827.

is supported by two central points. The first pertains to the need to clarify how the practical impact of authoritative orders differs from ordinary reasons for action.[44] Raz suggests a characterization of this difference in terms of the thesis according to which orders are not just reasons that may override other reasons; they are exclusionary reasons, reasons for not acting on other reasons. I have already shown, in my discussion of the duty and command components, that the difference between authoritative commands and ordinary reasons for action may be clarified in different terms altogether.[45]

The second point with which Raz supports his argument has to do with what he calls the "normal justification" for acknowledging authority.

the normal way to establish that a person has authority over another person involves showing that the alleged subject is likely better to comply with reasons which apply to him...if he accepts the directives of the alleged authority as authoritatively binding and tries to follow them, rather than by trying to follow the reasons which apply to him directly.[46]

Authorities, according to Raz, are subject to the normative principle mentioned above. The contents of their instructions should be based on the reasons according to which their subjects should act. He terms this "the dependence thesis."[47] The normal justification for authorities, and the dependence thesis lead Raz to the conclusion that acknowledging an authority involves refraining from action based on reasons relating to the contents of its instructions. Your acceptance of someone's authority implies a belief, on your part, that following his or her instructions will afford you more success, in keeping with the reasons for which you should act. In acting on these reasons both directly and because of the authority's instructions, you are committing the sin of a double counting of the same set of reasons.[48] In

---

[44] See Raz, *The Morality of Freedom*, p. 41.
[45] See pp. 20–1, 23–4 and note 24 above.
[46] Raz, *The Morality of Freedom*, p. 53. Two clarifications should be made here. First, the normal justification for authority mentioned in the text is, according to Raz's view, only part of the full justification for acknowledging authority. Such a full justification must not only show that there are reasons for accepting the authority in question, but also that there are no reasons not to accept it. For instance, it is desirable for people to manage their own lives. In order that authority be recognized on a given matter, it must be shown that this consideration doesn't apply (*ibid.*, pp. 56–7). Second, the normal justification for authority being what it is, Raz believes that it doesn't apply in the context of the institutions of state and law regarding all matters and all citizens. He believes that the state and the law do not have authority over all citizens in all matters (*ibid.*, ch. 4).   [47] *Ibid.*, p. 47.
[48] *Ibid.*, p. 58.

other words, the obligatory force of an authority's instructions stems from the reasons that justify them. Treating its instructions as reasons should thus replace the reasons that justify its instructions in the first place. Once we have acknowledged the authority, we should no longer act directly on these reasons.[49]

Raz is of the opinion that this argument is true not only of authorities' successful instructions but also of their mistaken ones. Even the failure of an authority's instructions to reflect the reasons on which a subject should act does not, he believes, allow the subject to take account of these reasons and disobey the instructions. This is so because "If every time a directive is mistaken, i.e. every time it fails to reflect reason correctly, it were open to challenge as mistaken, the advantage gained by accepting the authority as a more reliable and successful guide to right reason would disappear."[50]

This claim is incorrect. Challenging some of an authority's instructions as mistaken, and even disobeying them, doesn't entail the disappearance of the advantages of acknowledging the authority as a reliable, successful guide to reasons for action. The decision whether or not to rely on someone as a guide to the correct reasons depends on the *chances* that his or her instructions will reflect these reasons, relative to the chances of the subject's acting on the same reasons in the absence of any mediation. The fact that the authority's subject discovers mistakes in its instructions means that in the case of these instructions the authority is not a good guide to action. Its future instructions' chances of proving better guides to action than the subject's direct, personal decisions, may also emerge, through this fact, as slimmer than the subject had thought. This does not mean that these chances are canceled altogether. In any case, it would be puzzling to think that these chances would remain unchanged were the subject to disregard the mistakes and do what he or she was told. Quite the opposite would seem to be the case.

What is needed here is just the distinction I discussed above, between professional authorities such as doctors and lawyers and the type of practical authorities of which the law is the central example. Raz's normal justification thesis applies to both types of authority. Acknowledging authorities of both types allows people to increase their chances of acting on just the reasons on which they should act. However, each type of authority increases these chances in a very

---

[49] *Ibid.*, p. 59.   [50] *Ibid.*, p. 61.

different way. The instructions of each type of authority consequently function in our practical thought in different ways.

Professional authorities help their subjects to do what they should through the advantage of their broader, more thorough knowledge of the relevant subject. Accordingly, acknowledging them means a willingness to forgo the *mental act* of considering the matter to which their instructions pertain. The subject of such an authority who goes to the trouble of deciding what to do on his or her own as regards each and every instruction loses the advantage gained by acknowledging the authority. This doesn't mean, however, that someone who happens to know an instruction to be mistaken is forbidden from relying on this knowledge as grounds for disobeying the instruction, or forbidden from actually disobeying it if it is indeed utterly mistaken. One can continue to enjoy the advantages of a professional authority even if he or she sometimes refrains from following its mistaken instructions.

Other types of practical authorities, of which the law is a central example, do not (at least for the most part) increase the chances that their subjects will act on just the reasons on which they should, through the relatively larger extent of their knowledge. They do so, instead, as they allow for the concretization of reasons on which one should act, reasons which would be difficult or impossible to act upon in the absence of such authority. Examples of this have been given above. If the payment of taxes were not ordained by the legal authorities, it would be difficult to attain the actualization of the value inherent in the existence of a public budget, a value well worth being realized. In order that each one of us have reason to act in the interests of this value, each of us must be sure that enough people are truly contributing towards its realization. A legal authority that issues instructions publicly and is capable of enforcing them, constitutes just such a guarantee. When the legal authority commands us to pay taxes, then, it helps us to do what we should, *not by informing us about an act of which we weren't aware, but by creating the conditions under which there is reason for doing what we knew anyway that we should do.* These conditions are created only by the instructions as determined by the authority. Subsequently, even if we think the contents of the tax regulations faulty, either in terms of justice or economically, we still have reason to obey them. There is no other way of attaining the goal of having a public budget. However, vis-à-vis our wish to attain this goal, and vis-à-vis our wish not to impair the future performance of the legal authority, in the interests of attaining future goals of this type, there is no reason not to examine the faults of the tax regulations as possible reasons for disobeying them, and even no reason not to disobey them if the faults are significant ones. Such acts of disobedience will not automatically cause the authority's collapse or the loss of the advantages it affords.

In attempting to argue the thesis according to which acknowledging an authority entails refraining from action for reasons that pertain to the substance of its instructions, Raz relies on more than just the two considerations cited above. He also employs a specific example of authority which lends attraction to his thesis: that of an arbitrator.[51] Subjecting ourselves to such an authority means that we cannot disobey its rulings on the basis of our objections to their contents.

The example of the arbitrator's authority indeed supports Raz's thesis, but it does so due to the unique justification for this type of authority. The support it lends the thesis is thus limited to authorities whose justification is of just this type. There are times when an authority should be acknowledged in order to end disputes and controversy. If someone's authority should, indeed, be recognized for this purpose, the parties who should recognize it cannot rely on their positions in the dispute as reasons for disobeying the authority. Such reliance constitutes a self-contradiction, and also foils, almost completely, any chances the authority has of settling future disputes that involve the disobedient party. One of the justifications for the law's authority is, in fact, the need to solve disputes. In instances where the law functions on the basis of this justification, its subjects are accordingly barred from relying on their objections to the substance of its instructions, as grounds for disobedience. However, as the fourth chapter will show in full detail the law's moral authority to settle disputes is a limited one. If the subject's objections to the contents of its instructions result from the fact that it oversteps these limits, its instruction merits exactly the same treatment that is given to any other instruction which is *ultra vires*: it is void (not from the legal point of view, but rather from that of the moral duty to obey the law). Thus, even when the acknowledgment of the law's authority entails one's surrender of the option of disobeying it for reasons following from its contents, the surrender in question is a very limited one. It certainly doesn't mean giving up the possibility of action based on unforeseen moral reasons.[52]

---

[51] *Ibid.*, p. 41.　　　　[52] See pp. 121–7; 151–2 below.

To summarize briefly, I have examined several truths regarding the concept of the duty to obey the law, which seemed, on the face of it, to entail the total surrender of a disobedience motivated by considerations following from the law's contents or circumstances of application. None of these in fact entails this conclusion. The anarchism which attempts to apprehend and reject this duty at the threshold of any moral debate, deeming it one that involves such a surrender by definition, is asking us to throw out the baby with the bath-water. Lest we find ourselves forced to abstain from independent and overall judgment of the law's contents, or from acting on such judgment, it instructs us to deny the duty to obey. I hope I have succeeded in showing that we can keep the baby and throw out the water. We can acknowledge obedience to the law as a duty, and still evaluate laws and even disobey them, if the reasons stemming from such evaluations override those supporting the duty to obey.

But are there in fact reasons supporting the duty to obey the law? My subsequent assumption is that this question may be answered in the affirmative. The history of thought from Plato's *Crito* to Rawls' *A Theory of Justice* is a record of unending attempts to supply the grounds for such an answer. And yet, as my introduction states, the last two decades have witnessed considerable criticism of these attempts, on the part of many philosophers, who claim that all of them have finally failed. These philosophers deny the duty to obey not because it is unfit to cross the threshold of morality, but because no moral values and principles in fact support it. In the next chapter I will try to show this view to be far too sweeping.

CHAPTER 2

The justifications for the duty to obey the law and critical anarchism

I have shown, in the previous chapter, that the duty to obey the law cannot be rejected outright as a moral impossibility. There is no contradiction between its acceptance and the independence of one's moral judgment and action. And yet, are there any moral grounds that justify this duty? Are there any moral reasons for adopting it? As I have already noted, the thought of the last two millennia has supplied this question with many affirmative answers, the success of which has been radically questioned by thinkers of the last two decades.

Two distinct types should be distinguished in the complex of reasons supporting the duty to obey, discussed in the course of the last two decades. The first includes reasons which arise only within the framework of democratic political systems. Reasons of the second type are not necessarily associated with such frameworks. For reasons that I shall explain at the beginning of the next chapter, I shall postpone my discussion of the first kind to that chapter. Here, I shall deal with the main general justifications for the duty to obey the law. There are six such justifications; the first is based on gratitude, another on consent, a third argument employs the possible negative consequences of disobedience, or in other words, the danger disobedience causes to the political system,[1] another argument is

---

[1] These three arguments in support of the duty to obey are already present in the writings of Plato: "Consider, Socrates, if we are speaking truly that in your present attempt you are going to do us an injury. For, having brought you into the world, and nurtured and educated you, and given you and every other citizen a share in every good which we had to give," the laws will tell Socrates, or so he at least believes as he and Crito examine the possibility of his escape from prison (Plato, *Crito*, 51). Moreover, he claims, they will say, "we further proclaim to any Athenian by the liberty which we allow him, that if he does not like us when he has become of age and has seen the ways of the city, and made our acquaintance, he may go where he pleases and take his goods with him. But he who has experience of the manner in which we order justice and administer the state, and still remains, has entered into an implied contract that he will do as we command him" (*ibid.*). For the Socratic formulation of the third argument, the argument from negative consequences, see the fourth section of this chapter (p. 66 below).

based on fairness and the next on the duty to support just institutions.[2] Recently, an additional argument has been offered, based on communal obligations.[3] The criticism aimed at the first two arguments is, in my opinion, fatal. Not so, however, the critiques of the arguments based on fairness, on negative consequences or on the duty to support just institutions. These, when joined by the argument based on communal obligations, continue, despite the criticism, to provide grounds for the duty to obey the law, albeit a somewhat weaker duty than is commonly believed. They support a duty that applies only to some rather than all of the acts ordained by law.

The criticism aimed at the arguments based on fairness, negative consequences and communal obligations, draws part of its effectiveness from the fact that each argument is taken on independently. Taken separately, these arguments are indeed far weaker than they are when conceived of as a complex whole. Though I too will discuss them separately, I will show how viewing them as a whole can supply answers to some of the points raised by their critics.

I. GRATITUDE

Most of us benefit considerably from the existence of a system of law. Some writers believe that this fact places us under an obligation of gratitude towards the government or the laws.[4] Obeying the law is conceived of as the appropriate expression of this gratitude, while disobeying it is viewed as ingratitude. This argument fails, as the fact that someone benefits from something isn't enough to place him or her under an obligation of gratitude. Moreover, the additional conditions necessary for the creation of such an obligation are not met, as we shall see shortly, in the context of the relations between the law and its subjects.

In the first place, in order that a beneficiary owe gratitude to his or her benefactor, the benefactor's act must be carried out with the intention of benefiting its receiver. Such an intention must form at least a significant portion of the benefactor's motivation. When we

---

[2] These are comparatively new arguments. The first was introduced into the debate on the duty to obey the law during the fifties, by Hart (see note 41 below), and was then further developed by Rawls (see note 42 below). The second began gaining recognition after Rawls' *A Theory of Justice* (see note 75 below).

[3] See Dworkin, *Law's Empire*, pp. 195–216.

[4] For a survey of the principle of gratitude see Simmons, *Moral Principles and Political Obligations*, p. 163 including notes; Soper, "The Obligation to Obey the Law" and Gans, "The Obligation to Obey the Law, Comment" in Gavison (ed.), *Issues in Contemporary Legal Philosophy*.

benefit from an act meant by its performer to benefit him or herself, or persons other than ourselves, we would seem to owe him or her nothing at all.[5] When I overhear and enjoy music that the neighbors are playing for their own enjoyment, I owe them no gratitude. The same goes for acts meant by their performer to benefit us, but motivated by previous obligations undertaken by the benefactor in his or her own interests.[6] When someone supplies us the goods he owes us according to a contract between us, we owe him no debt of gratitude, as his intention to supply us with goods originates in the obligation he has undertaken in his own interests. In other words, altruistic motivation on the part of the benefactor is a necessary condition for his or her right to the beneficiary's gratitude. This condition is not met in the case of the goods supplied us by a system of laws.

The benefactor, in this candidate for a gratitude relationships, may be identified in various ways. None of these, however, makes it possible to credit the benefactor with altruistic motives. Socrates' stance in the *Crito*, intimates one way in which the benefactor may be identified. He personifies the laws themselves, subsequently assigning them the characteristics of a merciful father upon whom his helpless children, the subjects, are completely dependent.[7] A second possible construal of the benefactor's identity may be based upon Hobbes' conception of law. This view sees the source of laws' validity as a personal one, locating it in the sovereign. Gratitude may thus be owed to the person in whom the laws' validity originates, and not to the personified laws. A third interpretation bears no relation either to

---

[5] Simmons, *Moral Principles and Political Obligations*, pp. 170–4, breaks this condition down into several components. He believes that in order for a benefactor to have a right to gratitude, the favor must be rendered with great effort or through exceptional sacrifice on his or her part; that it must be rendered intentionally, voluntarily and for the beneficiary's good. This is correct. However, the stipulation that in order for the beneficiary to owe gratitude it is necessary for the benefactor to act out a specific intention to benefit this beneficiary seems to me to presuppose the conditions of intention and voluntariness. As to the first condition of special effort on the part of the benefactor: it is not clear whether the stipulation that the benefactor's act must involve special effort presupposes that the beneficiary's good is the reason for this act, or vice versa. In any case, there is some amount of redundancy in Simmons' discussion.

[6] The question when conduct resulting from prior duties is worthy of gratitude and when it isn't is also discussed by Simmons in highly interesting and important detail (*ibid.*, pp. 179–83). I see my discussion in the text as providing an answer, to some extent, to this question. Behavior arising from a duty that someone has originally undertaken from altruistic motives is behavior which entitles this person to gratitude. Behavior arising from a duty undertaken by someone in his or her own interests is not worthy of gratitude. The fact that egotistical and altruistic motives often lead to the selfsame actions and jointly bring people to undertake certain duties is one that usually complicates the answer to the question whether or not the gratitude is owed for these actions.   [7] Plato, *Crito*, 51.

a personifying metaphysics or to a personalistic conception of the laws' source of validity. Instead, it emphasizes the fact that laws are created and operated by human beings, arguing that our debt of gratitude is owed to the people who take the trouble to enact and enforce the laws.[8]

As stated, none of these versions of the benefactor's identity allays the criticism of the gratitude argument as failing to meet the condition of altruistic motivation. The Socratic position is the weakest one. It seems metaphysically undesirable to personify laws (what metaphysical consideration would justify a conception of laws as the same type of entities that humans are?), while the merciful character Socrates assigns this metaphysical embarrassment presupposes just what it sets out to prove. It is rather difficult to ascribe altruistic intentions to laws, not because there is any evidence to the contrary, but because it is difficult to ascribe them any intentions at all.

The possibility that we owe gratitude to the person in whom the laws' validity originates, and not to the laws themselves, is one that has no metaphysical flaws. Its flaws are, rather, jurisprudential. It was rejected long ago by theoreticians of law.[9] Even if it were true that the laws' validity originated in a flesh-and-blood human being, it would be quite difficult to attribute altruistic motivation as regards the laws' enactment and enforcement, to the personage in question. According to the Hobbesean model this is definitely impossible, as one of its basic assumptions is that the individual motives of the sovereign, like those of all human agents, are egotistical.

The third interpretation too, according to which gratitude is owed to the actual people enacting and enforcing the laws, under their natural capacities as humans, is plagued by the absence of altruistic motivation. Even when altruistic motivation can be discerned in the representatives and the appointees enacting and enforcing laws, it would be extremely reckless to treat this as the dominant factor motivating their conduct as legislators and law enforcers. If their motives have to do, for the most part, with self-interest or prior obligations taken on in their own interests, then no gratitude is owed them.[10]

---

[8] Simmons, *Moral Principles and Political Obligations*, ch. 7, mentions such an interpretation. It is also prominent in Soper, "The Obligation to Obey the Law."

[9] On the personalistic model of the legal system, a model originating in Hobbes and developed by Bentham and Austin, see Hart, *The Concept of Law*, ch. 4; Raz, *The Concept of a Legal System*, chs. 1–2.

[10] And if indeed there are some of them that do much more than required by self-interest or by duties undertaken in their own interests, then they deserve a gratitude that obeying the

Some philosophers are not content with this fatal criticism of the attempt to base the duty to obey on an obligation of gratitude. They point out additional flaws in this endeavor. First, they note that in order that an obligation of gratitude apply, altruistic motivation on the part of the benefactor is not enough. What is required is also the beneficiary's acceptance of the benefit of his or her own free will. The beneficiary must prefer, at least to some extent, receiving the benefits while suffering the loss caused through the acts expressing his or her gratitude, to a situation lacking both.[11] This condition may be met in the case of many of the law's subjects, but it certainly isn't met in all cases. Not all of the law's subjects have good reason to prefer the situation combining the advantages and disadvantages of obedience and of the law's existence, to one where neither exist. We could correctly say of some that the goods granted them by the law are in fact forced upon them. Someone who receives goods inadvertently owes no debt of gratitude to their giver, even when the latter acts on purely altruistic motives.

It should be noted that the first objection to the attempt to derive the duty to obey from the obligation of gratitude casts doubt upon the very applicability of such an obligation to the relations between the law and its subjects. The present objection, on the other hand, casts doubt upon the universality of this obligation's applicability.

However, let's assume that the obligation of gratitude applies to the relations between the law and its subjects. Even then, some critics claim, it would still not entail the duty to obey the law. The weakness they point out pertains to the question whether or not obeying the law is indeed the appropriate way to express such gratitude. Their answer is negative. If, they claim, the law's subjects do indeed have an obligation of gratitude towards it, then there are a multitude of ways for expressing this gratitude, besides obeying the law. They could volunteer for other activities that would serve the system, contribute portions of their money or time, etc.[12]

law cannot express, as it will not suffice to distinguish between those of the law's enactors and operators who deserve this special thanks and those who don't. On the question whether obeying the law should at all constitute a way of expressing gratitude, see below in the text.

[11] The benefactor's identity may form a component of this preference. For instance, someone may desire certain goods on the condition that they be supplied by A and not by B. In our context, someone may desire specific goods, received due to the existence of a system of laws if this system of laws is of one, rather than another, nature. Simmons mentions this condition and elaborates further on the condition cited in the text, that of preferring the situation that includes the goods to the one from which they are lacking. See Simmons, *Moral Principles and Political Obligations*, pp. 175–8.

[12] See Smith, "Is There a *Prima Facie* Obligation to Obey the Law?". He claims that even if obeying the law is the most successful way of expressing gratitude, the duty to express

The critics who choose to emphasize this point rely on the general problem raised by the issue of determining the acts a person should perform in order to express gratitude. The relations within which such obligations arise are usually varied and complex enough to make it unwise to identify a specific act or group of acts in advance, as those whose performance should express gratitude. Though I agree, in general, I see this as a less problematic point in the context of the legal system–subject relationship. As I see it, were there indeed an obligation of gratitude owed by the subjects to the system, some of the best candidates for expressing such gratitude would be acts that fall within the category of obedience to the law. Many acts of obedience are necessary for the very existence of the legal system, a

gratitude nonetheless doesn't entail the duty to express gratitude in the most convincing way. "A person with demanding, domineering parents might best display his gratitude towards them by catering to their every whim, but he surely has no *prima facie* obligation to do so" (pp. 953–4). The question, however, is not whether we should express gratitude in the most convincing way, but whether in the case where someone owes gratitude to another, a given action or type of actions may be selected as the most suitable for expressing this gratitude. In the case of the relationship between the law and its subjects, the group of actions of obeying the law is a suitable candidate, and it is one precisely because it is not the most convincing group of actions. Actions beyond obedience to the law, various types of voluntary actions, would give the most convincing expression of gratitude to the laws or to those behind them, were these worthy of gratitude. Obedience to the law is the minimum, then. It is for this reason and due to the (comparatively) easily discernible limits of the type of actions included under such obedience, that it seems especially suitable as a candidate for expressing gratitude, or at least a lack of ingratitude, towards the state. Smith's example of yielding to parents' whims is even somewhat misleading. Again, the question that should be asked is not whether yielding to their whims is the best way to express gratitude towards them, but whether the type of actions whose performance is demanded or requested by them, and not necessarily their whimsical demands, should indeed be the group of actions through which gratitude to them ought to be expressed. An affirmative answer to this question doesn't entail the conclusion that parents' whims should be yielded to. It only entails the conclusion that the fact that a given action is requested by parents is a reason for performing it, but not a decisive reason. If the contents of the request are of a whimsical nature, we may finally decide not to fulfill it, although this is the request of our parents and we believe that this fact should support the performance of the stipulated acts. Simmons is aware of the possibility of this type of reply (see Simmons, *Moral Principles and Political Obligations*, p. 186). He points out that obedience to the law is needed by the government and that it will not be able to exist in the absence of such obedience, but he claims that the fact that given actions on our part will allow for the existence of an object to which we owe gratitude does not entail that we are indeed duty-bound to perform this action as an expression of the gratitude in question. He offers the example of a person in need of dialysis and asks whether, in case we owe this person our gratitude, we are duty-bound to pay for the dialysis machine, its daily operation, etc. The answer that should be made to Simmons in the context of this example is identical to the one that Smith should have been given regarding the example of parents' whims. If we owe someone our gratitude and if this person is in need of dialysis in order to live, this fact clearly gives us a *prima facie* reason to express such gratitude through efforts to secure the dialysis. Clearly, when the item in question is an expensive one such as a dialysis machine, strong considerations may oppose this manner of expressing our gratitude. It all depends, among other things, upon our means.

fact well worth considering when determining the ways for expressing gratitude. The obligation of gratitude is an obligation owed to someone who has benefited you out of altruistic motives. Accordingly, thanks to such a benefactor should be expressed in the light of his, her or its special needs. However, not all acts of obedience to the law would be suitable candidates for expressing gratitude. As we shall see below, not every act of obedience to the law is necessary to the system or important to it.[13]

The obligation of gratitude, then, were it to entail the duty to obey, would entail it not as a universal duty (not only in the sense that it would not apply to all of the system's subjects, but also in the sense of failing to create reasons for obeying all the acts ordained by law). As I have already claimed, and will demonstrate in detail below, this lack of universality doesn't mean that any reference to the duty to obey the law is mistaken or superfluous. However, the argument presently in question doesn't justify this duty in any case. Altruistic motives on the part of the benefactor are a necessary condition for the existence of a debt of gratitude to him or her, and such motives, as I have already shown, cannot be ascribed to the system of laws or to the people behind it.

Perhaps, though, behind the laws are neither a personal sovereign nor those who enact and operate them, but rather all of the individuals who take it upon themselves to obey the law in order that it may exist. As the existence of a system of laws provides us with various important goods, perhaps we owe our obedience to all those subjects whose obedience allows for the system's existence, even though their motives may not be altruistic? This attempt to support the duty to obey focuses on the mutual relations between the law's subjects, rather than the relationship between the subjects and the law, the source of its validity, or its operators. It is more than anecdotal that this focus is adopted by the very thinker whose theory of the concept of law persistently replaces the Hobbesian personal model of the law with an impersonal one. H. L. A. Hart tells us that in disobeying the law we are not acting unfairly towards it or the person generating its validity; we are not acting unfairly towards the law's operators. We are acting unfairly towards our fellow members of society – towards the rest of the law's subjects. I shall discuss this argument in the third part of this chapter, as it originates not only in

---

[13] See below, section 4, pp. 71–4.

the gratitude argument but also in the argument based on consent, which I will now proceed to address.

2. CONSENT

The most popular attempt in the history of endeavors to justify the duty to obey the law is probably the one which relies on the consent of the law's subjects. Consent is considered the most typical, undisputable source of obligations. Many have assumed that success in demonstrating that the law's subjects have consented to obey it would serve to justify the duty to obey firmly and decisively. It is difficult to point out an explicit expression of consent to obey the law on the part of all or most of its subjects.[14] Conversely, the arguments in favor of the duty to obey are aimed at the justification of its universal or nearly universal applicability. This clash has led many philosophers to ascribe consent to obey to the law's subjects, in many different ways, even though no such consent has been expressed by them explicitly.

Some point out the actual conduct of all or most of the subjects of systems of laws, conduct such as continued residence in a given locale, or voting for its legislative body. They cite such conduct as indicative of these subjects' consent to obey the laws of the place in question. Some claim that actual, albeit implicit, consent could be inferred from such conduct.[15] Others hold that no such actual consent can be inferred, but consider at least one of these modes of conduct, i.e. voting, to merit treatment *as if* it expressed such consent ("quasi-consent").[16] Some recourse to hypothetical consent[17] rather than actual (past or present) conduct.[18] This consent, as opposed to the former, is not inferred from the subjects' conduct. It follows from principles thought by this argument's supporters to apply to the subjects, principles according to which they should consent to obey.

[14] Explicit consent can only be pointed out on the part of small and exclusive groups such as state officials or naturalized immigrants. On the duty to obey of the latter, and their explicit consent, see Sartorius, "Political Authority and Political Obligation"; A. J. Simmons, "Voluntarism and Political Associations," *Virginia Law Review* 67 (1981), 19; Greenawalt, *Conflicts of Law and Morality*, pp. 77–80.

[15] The major contender for this view is of course Locke. See note 25 below.

[16] See Singer, *Democracy and Disobedience*, pp. 47–53.

[17] The arguments from historical and hypothetical consent should be distinguished from the arguments from tacit consent and quasi-consent. Tacit consent is based on actual conduct revealing actual consent; the argument from quasi-consent progresses from actual conduct to normative results identical to those of consent, and not to actual consent. On the other hand, the arguments from historical and hypothetical consent are not only not arguments for actual consent, neither are they arguments from actual conduct.

[18] For instance, Thomas Hobbes in *Leviathan* and John Rawls in *A Theory of Justice*.

Some, rather than basing the duty to obey on the consent of the law's individual subjects, try to base it on an historic consent, that of the first generation of subjects to a given system of laws.[19]

The last two versions of the consent argument should be rejected nearly outright. There are two central elements in the complex forming the justification according to which consent is an undisputable source of obligations. First, the fact of consent, the fact that someone has actually acted in a manner expressing consent, is a fact that creates expectations and reliances in other people. Second, the fact of (freely given) consent, means that these expectations and reliances were willed and created intentionally. The creation of expectations and reliances due to the fact of consent, and the fact that their creation was intentional and willed, form necessary and prominent parts of the explanation of consent's attraction as a basis for obligations. The attempt to ground the duty to obey in hypothetical consent, and the attempt to base it on historical consent, both postulate a consent devoid of these two crucial components.

Hypothetical consent is not actual consent (and unlike quasi-consent it isn't even based on actual conduct). If expectations and reliances can be referred to at all in the context of such a consent, they cannot result from the fact that it has been given, but from the validity of the principle according to which it should be given. It would thus be incorrect to cite the consent in question as the source of these expectations and reliances. They should arise whether or not consent is actually given. Their appearance must accordingly be attributed directly to the principle due to which consent should be given, not to the fact of consent itself. Now, the fact that I should give my consent doesn't mean that I have consented, that I actually choose and wish to perform the act of consent. We are thus faced with a consent from which the suitable element of free will is also absent.[20]

Besides incorporating what is, to a large extent, a far-fetched

---

[19] Richard Hooker, one of the first thinkers of modern times (late sixteenth century) who attempted to ground political obligation and authority on the consent of their subjects, speaks expressly of historical consent (*Of the Laws of Ecclesiastical Polity* [Cambridge: Cambridge University Press, 1989], pp. 87–9). Such consent is also intimated by Hobbes and Rousseau. See Simmons, *Moral Principles and Political Obligations*, p. 60. On historical consent, see also Greenawalt, *Conflicts of Law and Morality*, p. 69.

[20] For somewhat different (and powerful) formulations of the criticism of the attempt to see hypothetical consent as a source of duties, see Sartorious, "Political Authority and Political Obligation," who refers to hypothetical consent in its Hobbesean sense, and also R. Dworkin, "The Original Position" in Norman Daniels (ed.), *Reading Rawls* (New York: Basic Books, 1975), pp. 17–18, who criticizes Rawls' version of hypothetical consent.

fiction,[21] the attempt to base the duty of all individuals at all times to obey the law on the actual consent given by the first generation is also one that proposes a consent bereft of these two crucial components. As the consent in question is not given by those who are under the obligations, it follows tautologically that the obligations it creates do not result from free choice on the part of these individuals and are not based on expectations and reliances created by them.[22]

In gauging the success of the attempt to base the duty to obey on consent, a special effort should be made to examine the thesis according to which the individual subjects express tacit or quasi-consent to obey a specific body of laws, through continued residence in a given locale or voting for its legislative bodies.[23] The following discussion will only ask whether or not residence in a given locale expresses tacit consent to obey its laws. Whether such consent may or may not be derived from the fact of voting, is a question that must be part of a discussion of the duty to obey the law within democratic political systems. I will accordingly discuss it in the third chapter.[24]

Locke, in *The Second Treatise of Civil Government*, says, "[E]very man, that hath possession, or enjoyment, of any part of the dominions of any government, doth thereby give his tacit consent, and is as far forth obliged to obedience to the laws of that government..."[25] Rousseau says, "When the State is instituted, residence constitutes consent; to dwell within its territory is to submit to the Sovereign."[26] This view precedes them in the teaching of Socrates,[27] and succeeds them in the thought of W. D. Ross.[28] All these writers construe the fact of residence in a given place as an expression of consent to obey the laws of this place, or as a form of conduct that should be treated as if it were such an expression.

Should people's residence or continued residence in a given place really be treated as an expression of consent to obey the laws of this place? There are two reasons for answering this in the negative. The

[21] On this see Hume, "Of the Original Contract" in Henry D. Aiken (ed.), *Hume's Moral and Political Philosophy* (New York: Hafner Press, 1948), p. 356.

[22] For a more detailed discussion see Simmons, *Moral Principles and Political Obligations*, pp. 60–1.

[23] To avoid confusion, I will comment here that I use the term "tacit consent" to denote what is usually denoted in the context of contract law by the expression "implied consent." The expression "quasi-consent" denotes, here, what is denoted in contract law by "estoppel by representation."   [24] See pp. 116–19 below.

[25] John Locke, *The Second Treatise of Civil Government* (Cambridge: Cambridge University Press, 1960), section 119.

[26] Rousseau, *The Social Contract* (London: Everyman, 1950), Book 4, ch. 2.

[27] Plato, *Crito*, 51.

[28] See W. D. Ross, *The Right and the Good* (Oxford: Oxford University Press, 1930), p. 27.

first is empirical: it just isn't true that people who continue to reside in specific places consent to obey the laws of these places, or create expectations that, as it were, indicate such consent. The second reason is normative: even if they were to consent, this should not be treated as a binding commitment, as their consent is given under duress.

People who continue to live in the place where they were born and raised are not aware that their continued residence there counts as consent, and do not intend it to be taken as such. As consent is an act involving a conscious and intentional mental act, and as most residents of most places have no memory of ever having performed such an act, it is empirically incorrect to claim that they have consented to obey the laws of their place of residence. This argument against the claim for consent, an argument presented as early as the eighteenth century by David Hume,[29] has lately been the subject of considerable controversy.

One writer has referred to the fact that unintentional consent is nonetheless binding at times. It is binding in cases where its giver, though unaware in point of fact of having given it, should have known that he or she was doing so. People who continue to live in countries after having matured politically, says Harry Beran, understand that in doing so they accept full membership in these countries. As a country is an organization bound by certain rules, and as people know full well what membership in such an organization means, they should understand that their acceptance of membership entails a duty to act by the organization's (or country's) rules. Failure to understand this is a result of carelessness. Not knowing something due to carelessness doesn't exempt one from the duty in question.[30]

A factual counter-claim may be used to answer Beran. It is not true that people conceive of the state in the same way that they view other familiar organizations. It also isn't true that they see themselves, in continuing their residence as adults in the places where they grew up, as accepting membership in an organization. Consequently, they cannot be said to show carelessness when they fail to conclude, from the fact that membership in an organization entails a willingness to keep its rules, that their continued residence in the place where they were raised means consent on their parts to obey its laws. This is the

[29] Hume, "Of the Original Contract."
[30] Beran, "In Defense of the Consent Theory of Political Obligation and Authority," *Ethics* 87 (1976–7), 260, p. 270.

answer Simmons[31] gives Beran and it is undoubtedly both correct and sufficient. More than this can, however, be said. Not only is it the case that people don't conceive of the state as an ordinary organization or of its laws as the rules of such an organization. The fact is, they shouldn't, and they also shouldn't be conceived of as viewing the state in this way. The reasons for this are fairly clear. Firstly, the state, unlike other organizations, sets out to control all aspects of life. Second, "membership" in the place where one was raised, unlike membership in other organizations, is difficult to end, besides which no one other than the individual member seems to have the right to end it. The last point takes us to the second argument for rejecting a view of residence as expressing tacit consent to the duty to obey the (given place's) law.

As stated, this argument holds that even if residents were to give their consent to obey the laws of their places of residence, by virtue of living there, this consent should not be considered a binding commitment. Having been given under duress, this consent is null. The choice assumed by an attempt to derive consent to obey a given place's law from continued residence in this place is a choice between emigration and continued residence there in combination with obedience. This is the choice cited by Socrates when he speaks for the laws of Athens,[32] and it is also the one assumed by Hume in his criticism of the present argument. According to Hume, the consent given by someone faced with this choice is not given freely, as the possibility of emigration is not a serious one for most of the state's subjects. His often quoted view on this subject is as follows:

Can we seriously say that a poor peasant or artisan has a free choice to leave his country, when he knows no foreign language or manners, and lives from day to day by the small wages which he acquires? We may as well assert that a man remaining in a vessel, freely consents to the dominion of the master, though he was carried on board while asleep, and must leap into the ocean and perish the moment he leaves her.[33]

This claim of Hume's is also debated by Beran and Simmons. According to Beran, Hume overlooks the distinction between a coerced choice and a difficult choice. The first is not binding. The second most certainly is.[34] For instance, someone who is forced at gun point to sell his or her business, at a tenth of its value, is not bound by

[31] A. J. Simmons, "Consent, Free Choice and Democratic Government," *Georgia Law Review* 18 (1984), 791, pp. 807–9.　　　　[32] Plato, *Crito*, 51.
[33] Hume, "Of the Original Contract," p. 363.
[34] H. Beran, "What is the Basis of Political Authority?," *Monist* 66 (1983), 487, pp. 497–8.

this consent of his or hers. This consent wasn't freely given and is thus invalid. On the other hand, someone who is forced to sell his or her property at a tenth of its value, to prevent a total financial collapse, is bound by this decision, despite the difficult choice with which he or she was faced.[35] Beran grants that emigration is a difficult choice. In his view, this does not make refraining from it and continued residence in combination with obeying the (given place's) law a choice made under duress.

Simmons admits the truth of these claims. He does not see a person's choice to continue living where they grew up, rather than emigrating, as one made under duress. However, he does not consider this choice to be a binding commitment. Though not made under duress, he views this as a choice made under undue influence. To demonstrate, he compares two cases. The first is that of a person forced to sell his or her property at a tenth of its value, to fend off financial disaster. In the second, a person agrees to a similar sale, to someone who is willing to save his or her life. Lost in the desert and dying of thirst, the owner agrees to sell all at a tenth of the property's value, to someone who will otherwise refuse to part with the glass of lemonade in his hand. The owner is not bound by this act of consent. True, he or she has not been forced to sell, unlike the person who sold at gun point. Unlike the case of selling due to financial difficulties, though, where Simmons only accuses the buyer of opportunism, the present case is one of exploitation. It is a case in which the seller's fundamental and necessary needs are being exploited.[36]

The distinction between difficult choices that frustrate consent, and difficult choices that do not, is quite common in the context of contract law. It would seem that the two cases described by Simmons do indeed fall on either side of the dividing line. His explanation for this doesn't seem very convincing though. It is hard to discern the line between mere opportunism and exploitation.[37] In any case, I do not intend to dwell on the issue, as I consider it unnecessary for the refutation of Beran's view. As I see it, Simmons gave in too soon in acknowledging people's choice to refrain from emigration as a difficult choice only, rather than a coerced one.

---

[35] The examples are Simmons'. See his "Consent, Free Choice and Democratic Government," pp. 811, 813.   [36] *Ibid.*, p. 815.

[37] In legal practice, decisions as to whether a given case of choice is difficult enough to nullify consent are often motivated by considerations of economic policy, and not by the existence of clear conceptual boundary lines. See A. Kronman, "Contract Law and Distributive Justice," *Yale Law Journal* 89 (1980), 472.

The question whether or not consent is freely given, whether it counts as coerced or not, isn't really answered in terms of the difficulties involved in one or more of the alternatives open to the chooser. Its answer depends much more on whether the party responsible for placing the chooser in a state where he or she is forced to choose between these alternatives is also the addressee of his or her consent. Judging whether the choice of the peasant, the artisan or any-one else, to stay where they live and obey, instead of emigrating, is or is not choice under coercion, doesn't depend that much on whether or not emigration is a difficult alternative. It depends much more on whether anyone, including the state, has a right to force us to choose either emigrating or staying and obeying. If the state has no such right, then people's consent to stay and obey instead of emigrating is not binding, just as such consent on their part would not be binding if they had been faced with a choice between this alternative and paying five pounds. Paying five pounds isn't particularly difficult for most people, but their choice to stay and obey just to avoid such a payment is not a binding one when it is directed towards whoever has forced them to make this choice, while having no right to do so.[38]

This central point is obscured by Hume's parable of the man on the boat (and in fact his concentration on the provincial peasant and artisan too). First, the parable stresses the insufferable difficulty of jumping into the ocean, more than it highlights the fact that the man made to choose between this jump and staying on board while obeying the owner has been brought aboard in his sleep, that is, unwillingly. Second, the parable omits an essential detail: it contains no answer to the question whether the agent who brought the sleeping man on board was the ship's owner, that is, the party now demanding the man's obedience or departure, or some other party. If it was the owner who brought him aboard in this manner, then the man's consent is not binding, not only because it was given under undue influence. It also isn't binding because it was given under duress.

In this context, the important question regarding the choice between emigrating and staying where one lives while obeying the laws is, why must we face a choice between these alternatives in the

---

[38] If we believe that consent to stay and obey, for the mere purpose of avoiding payment of five pounds, nonetheless creates a duty, this is not because the consent to obey seems valid. It is, rather, because we think that someone who preferred staying and obeying to paying five pounds and disobeying, is worthy of punishment for his folly.

first place? Why can't we choose both, that is, stay rather than emigrate, and fail to obey as well? It would seem that we won't choose both in one case only – if the state forces us to select a single alternative. However, in order that the choice of one of these alternatives may count as free, it must be shown that the state has a right to force its residents to choose only one of the alternatives and not both.

One way of demonstrating that the state has such a right is through arguing that there is a duty to obey the state. For the purposes of the present discussion, though, such a claim clearly begs the question. The argument from consent is intended to prove the existence of such a duty, for which reason it is impossible to assume its existence for the purposes of this argument. There may be other ways of showing that the state has a right to make us choose between emigration and continued residence in combination with obedience. So far, however, none of those who have presented residence as an expression of tacit consent to obey the law of the land have suggested any such ways.

In short, perhaps the choice between emigration and staying and obeying is indeed a difficult one, and perhaps the consent it produced isn't valid, partly because it is given under undue influence. This is not all though. This consent is disqualified mainly because it is given under duress. It would seem that one who puts such a choice to us is forcing it on us, with no right to do so. It not only doesn't bind us when we are poor, uni-lingual, provincial peasants or artisans. It also doesn't bind us when we are wealthy, multi-lingual cosmopolitans either. Simmons' mistake when he accedes to Beran's objection to Hume follows from the fact that he likens the state in which people face a choice between emigration and continued residence combined with obedience, to a state in which someone faces a choice between dying of thirst and trading his property for a tenth of its value and a glass of lemonade. The analogue better suited to the choice described by those who claim that continued residence means tacit consent to obey is that of someone who takes someone else's canteen in the desert, and then gives him the choice of either not getting it back and dying of thirst, or getting it back in return for his property at a tenth of its worth. The owner of the canteen is entitled to have it back without selling his property. His consent to accept it only if he sells his possessions is not only consent under undue influence, but also under duress, and it is chiefly due to this that it doesn't hold.

Does the failure of the attempt to base the duty to obey the law on consent mean that this duty cannot be based on the wills of its supposed subjects? The attempt to base the duty to obey on fairness, discussed in the following section, is to a large extent an examination of this question.[39] As stated at the end of the previous section, the argument from fairness is also related to the one examined by that section, i.e. the argument from gratitude.[40]

3. FAIRNESS

When a number of persons conduct any joint enterprise according to rules and thus restrict their liberty, those who have submitted to these restrictions when required have a right to a similar submission from those who have benefited by their submission. The rules may provide that officials should have authority to enforce obedience ... but the moral obligation to obey the rules in such circumstances is due to the cooperating members of the society, and they have the correlative moral right to obedience.

Both H. L. A. Hart, whose formulation this is,[41] and John Rawls, who termed this " the principle of fairness " and developed it further,[42] consider it a basis for the duty to obey the law.

Implicit in the discussions of some of the writers who examine the argument for the duty to obey based on this principle is a conception of it as what, in Aristotelian terms, would be called an argument of corrective justice.[43] As such, its central fundamental assumption is

---

[39] Soper points out the affinity between the argument from fairness and the argument from consent (see Soper, "The Obligation to Obey the Law," pp. 135–40). This affinity is also hinted in H. L. A. Hart, "Are There Any Natural Rights?," *Philosophical Review* 64 (1955), 175, p. 185, and Robert Nozick, *Anarchy, State and Utopia* (Oxford: Basil Blackwell, 1974), pp. 90–5. The principle of fairness is largely similar to the principle underlying the field of law known as "quasi-contract law." The deliberations as to whether or not this principle succeeds in supporting this duty are, in turn, similar to those involved in delineating the duties created by quasi-contracts. Quasi-contract law is closely related to the legal field of contract law, a field dealing with the creation of obligations through consent. The affinity between the attempt to base obedience to the law on the principle of fairness, and the attempt to base it on consent, is thus largely analogous to the affinity between quasi-contract law and contract law.

[40] The affinity between the argument from fairness and the argument from gratitude is emphasized in Smith, "Is There a *Prima Facie* Obligation to Obey the Law?," p. 945.

[41] Hart, "Are There Any Natural Rights?," p. 185.

[42] His discussion of the principle of fairness is, mainly, to be found in "Legal Obligation and the Duty of Fair Play" in Sidney Hook (ed.), *Law and Philosophy* (New York: New York University Press, 1964). He also deals with fairness in *A Theory of Justice*, pp. 342–50, and in other places. For a full list see Simmons, *Moral Principles and Political Obligations*, p. 214, note 5.

[43] For instance, Smith, "Is There a *Prima Facie* Obligation to Obey the Law?"; Soper, "The Obligation to Obey the Law"; and to some extent also Arenson, "The Principle of Fairness and Free-Rider Problems," *Ethics* 92 (1982), 616, pp. 632–3.

that someone who has received goods as a result of others' activities
must pay their price even if he or she did not order them. However,
this may also be conceived of as an argument of distributive justice.[44]
It should, in fact, be conceived of as this alone.[45] As such, its central

---

[44] The most detailed discussions of the principle of fairness indeed conceive of it in this way. I'm
referring to Simmons, *Moral Principles and Political Obligations*, pp. 101–42, and Greenawalt,
Conflicts of Law and Morality, pp. 121–58, though Simmons sometimes replaces the distributive
justice view of the principle of fairness with one that conceives it in terms of corrective justice.
On this point see chapter 3, below, pp. 102–3.

[45] There are two central reasons due to which the fairness principle should not be understood
as a principle of corrective justice, in the context of an attempt to use it as grounds for the
duty to obey the law. When understood as a principle of corrective justice, it commands
those who have received goods as a result of the activities of others to pay the price of these
goods. As a source for the duty to obey the law, this principle may emerge as useless, for one
may pose the question already asked of the attempt to derive the duty to obey from the
principle of gratitude: why does fairness require obeying the law as the price that one is
obliged to pay for goods received through others' activities which maintain the legal system?
As stated, in the argument from gratitude, obedience to the law forms the suitable way to
express gratitude as it is specifically such obedience that is needed by the benefactor, i.e. by
the legal system, in order to exist, and as this fact should be taken into account in determining
how to express the gratitude in question. I have already argued that it should be taken into
account, as the duty of gratitude is one which we owe someone whom altruistic motives lead
to benefit us. Accordingly, recompensation should be made with special attention to the
benefactor's needs. However, in the context of the principle of fairness, unlike that of
gratitude, the duty of recompensation exists even if our benefactor has not benefited us with
the purpose of serving our interests. Thus, the character of the goods received, rather than
the needs of their giver, should determine the nature of the recompensation. When the
greengrocer who has laid a basket of vegetables at my doorstep is urgently in need of a baby-
sitter, this is only of special weight in determining how to repay him for the vegetables I have
consumed, if he has supplied them knowing my own needs and making a special attempt to
serve them of themselves. If he left the vegetables at my doorstep in order to promote sales,
then the fact that he suddenly needs a baby-sitter is of no special weight in determining how
to repay him. In short, even if those who enjoy the goods created by the legal system were
obliged by fairness to make recompensation for these goods, it is not at all clear that they
would be obliged to do so by obeying the law.
    Second, and I consider this objection more important than the previous one, even if
obedience to the law were the appropriate manner of repayment for goods received by virtue
of the existence of a legal system, the very need to argue this would indicate that a central
point of the argument from fairness had been missed altogether. It seems that if the
conception of the principle of fairness as grounds for the duty to obey the law is such that it
forces us to turn on considerations outside this principle, in order to explain why it is
obedience to the law which is required by the principle, then something of importance has
been lost, whether or not any such considerations may be offered. For it would seem that in
the context of the argument of fair play, the duty to participate in the goods' creation is far
more intimate. It would seem that this duty is in no need of intermediary normative
considerations lying outside of the principle of fairness. It seems an organic part of the
principle itself. This is at least intimated by the spirit of Hart's and Rawls' discussions. I shall
again quote Hart's formulation of the principle of fairness: "When a number of persons
conduct any joint enterprise according to rules and thus restrict their liberty, those who have
submitted to these restrictions when required have a right to *a similar submission* from those
who have benefited by their submission" (italics mine). This intimate link between the duty
to participate in the goods' creation and the enjoyment of their existence, can only be an
expression of the distributive justice view of the principle of fairness.

fundamental assumption is that if the production of goods open to
public consumption depends upon the burdens borne by at least some
of the individuals forming this public, then these burdens should be
divided equally between all of the consumers capable of participating
in the production process.

Robert Nozick used the following example to question this
argument.[46] A group of neighbors cooperate on the institution of a
public entertainment center in their neighborhood. The center is
designed to entertain them in their homes. Most of the neighborhood's residents contribute towards its establishment, and all of them
enjoy its benefits upon opening their windows. Nozick points out that
it is not at all obvious that all of the residents can be said to be
consuming the center's entertainment of their own free will. The
central motive causing some of the residents to open their windows
may possibly be access to fresh air. They simply consume the
entertainment as they can't not consume it (except by paying the
excessively uncomfortable price of leaving their windows shut or
stopping up their ears). In other words, Nozick believes it possible
that some of the residents, though they benefit from the entertainment, might prefer living without it and not sharing the burden
of its upkeep, to sharing these burdens and enjoying the entertainment. These residents will not, according to Nozick, be bound to
participate in the institution and upkeep of the center. The only ones
obligated to do so are those who consented to its establishment in the
first place. Subsequently, the principle of fairness is either swallowed
up by the uncontroversial principle that agreements must be fulfilled,
or proves no obligation whatsoever. This means the complete
cancellation of the principle of fairness as an independent source of
obligations, including the duty to obey the law.

Nozick's example has a lot of charm and truth to it, but not quite
the whole truth. What bothers us about this example, as Nozick
himself emphasizes, is the fact that in demanding that someone pay
the price of the entertainment, we are in danger of demanding him or
her to pay for goods that he or she might rather not have, and not pay
for, than consume and pay for.[47] Allowing this would mean, among
other things, allowing people unlimited and manipulative inter-
ference in each other's priorities, carried out by heaping each other
with unsought goods. And yet, in order to avoid this consequence, it

---

[46] Nozick, *Anarchy, State and Utopia*, p. 93.   [47] *Ibid.*, p. 94.

isn't necessary to agree with Nozick and reject the principle of fairness altogether.

As John Simmons has claimed, if people willingly consume given benefits, then fairness requires that they pay for them, even if they haven't consented to such an arrangement in advance.[48] Let's say, for instance, that the residents of the building where I live get together and invest in a T.V. antenna tuned to distant stations. If I make use of the reception options made possible by this antenna, then I may justifiably be said to be consuming the benefits provided by this antenna of my own free will. I have the option of enjoying these benefits (granted, through others' efforts), but in contrast to the case of Nozick's entertainment center, I also have the option of not enjoying them. Thus, if I take advantage of the opportunity to enjoy them, fairness requires that I pay for these benefits. Simmons, then, as opposed to Nozick, claims, and justly so, that the principle of fairness can be a source of obligation, independently of consent. It is a source of obligation in cases where someone enjoys benefits of his or her own free will, though not having agreed in advance to receive them.[49]

Nonetheless, Simmons agrees with Nozick that the principle of fairness cannot supply a basis for the duty to obey the law. As stated, the principle of fairness applies only to goods that we wish to consume. It doesn't apply to goods that we consume without wishing to. In the case of goods such as the antenna, what we are dealing with are clearly goods that are willingly consumed. This is so as they are consumed while there is a choice of either doing so or not. However, in the case of goods which we cannot choose not to consume, such as those supplied by Nozick's entertainment center, it is not at all clear that we wish to consume them.

The goods afforded us as a result of the existence of a system of laws are clearly of the latter type. These are goods which we cannot choose not to consume, just like those of the entertainment center example. Can it be said that we wish to consume the goods produced by the

---

[48] Simmons, *Moral Principles and Political Obligations*, pp. 118–36. See also Sartorious, "Political Authority and Political Obligation," pp. 12–13.

[49] *Ibid.* It seems that considerations of this type are also the central considerations guiding the field of legal obligations known as quasi-contract law. (See note 39 above.) If the local greengrocer leaves a basket of vegetables on my doorstep, unasked, and I take it in and eat the vegetables, I am in debt under a quasi-contract. Conversely, if the local painter paints the exterior of my house, unasked, I owe him nothing, even if I don't bother to remove the paint, even if I enjoy the fact that my home is newly painted.

law, despite the fact that we consume them without having chosen to do so?

Simmons' claim that the duty to obey the law cannot be based on fairness is grounded, for the most part, on his negative reply to this question.[50] When will goods produced through others' cooperation, which we consume without having chosen to do so, count as goods which we wish to consume? According to Simmons, this cannot happen when we view these goods as having been forced upon us, or as not being worth the price we are asked to pay for them. This condition is not met, he claims, in the case of many of those for whom the principle of fairness is supposed to justify the duty to obey the law. Many of the law's subjects view the goods it produces as having been forced upon them, or at least as not being worth the price they are made to pay for them.

To me, this empirical claim seems a curious one. The goods we receive as a result of the existence of a system of laws include, as we shall see in detail further on,[51] the very existence of this system as a tool for the institution and enforcement of desirable behavior, as well as the social stability and certainty that its existence produces.[52]

---

[50] He also bases it on the non-fulfillment of another condition which he considers necessary for the application of the duty of fair play. According to this condition, a person is not required, by fair play, to bear the burdens of a communal endeavor creating benefits which he enjoys, if he isn't aware that these benefits are created by this communal endeavor. In Simmons' view, people are not aware that the benefits created by the law and enjoyed by them are created through the cooperation of their fellow community members. Most people believe that they purchase these benefits from the government to which they pay their taxes. It is difficult to see how this claim might be supported. In the next part of the chapter I shall deal with goods created by the law which are relevant to the application of the principle of fairness. Here, however, I shall ask: is the operation of the legal and governmental system as an institution deciding public disputes or solving coordination problems, actually a good which may be maintained by paying taxes? Isn't it clear that the abstention of objectors from acting on their views when these contradict those of the government is a burden that must be carried in order to allow the government to be the institution that decides controversial issues, and that those living in the community are or should be aware of this fact? Is not the functioning of the law in solving problems of coordination made possible through the very willingness of many to obey it? Moreover, could the more specific goods created by certain laws – for instance, a sense of personal safety, ecological conservation, town planning, etc. – be produced entirely through the threat of punishment by a system of enforcement fed by taxes, in which no burdens of obedience are borne due to the cooperation of many of society's members? On this matter, and on the motives and knowledge due to which the principle of fairness will bind society members to bear the burdens allowing for the goods' creation, see the detailed and excellent discussion in Greenawalt, *Conflicts of Law and Morality*, pp. 127–8, 133–6.   [51] See below, pp. 67–70.

[52] Simmons' factual thesis seems to be based on many people's view of their obedience to laws imposing large taxes or military service in policing activities in foreign lands, etc. as inappropriate compensation for the goods awarded them by the law. The rule of law, the protection of the armed forces, control of environmental pollution, maintenance of a traffic

People have strong selfish reasons (given such powerful philosophical expression by Thomas Hobbes) for preferring a situation in which a system of laws exists and they obey it, to one where neither is the case, and selfish reasons play a central part in human action. True, people are sometimes blind to what serves their own interests, but blindness regarding the present matter is extremely rare. This is testified to by the widespread popularity of aphorisms of the type of the Talmudic "Were it not for the fear of government, man would swallow his brother," and the Hobbesian observation that without government, "life is solitary, poor, nasty, brutish and short." There would seem to be solid grounds for the hypothesis that, contrary to Simmons' view, most people prefer a situation in which laws are kept to one in which they aren't, even if they are required, in the first, to pay the price of obedience (subject to the limits discussed later on), a price from which they are exempted in the latter.[53]

In the context of the law, then, people may be said to prefer the law's existence and obedience to it, to the absence of both. It consequently seems that, in this case, the principle of fairness can serve as a basis for the duty to obey. Moreover, it seems that the principle of fairness also applies to cases other than those in which people desire the existence of institutions or given states of affairs as a matter of their personal inclinations or interests. The principle of fairness can produce obligations to share the burdens required for the existence of institutions and states of affairs which people consider necessary from a moral point of view.[54] I will illustrate with an example. The air pollution in a given town approaches a deadly

---

system, etc., do not seem to them worth the price. (See, *Moral Principles and Political Obligations*, p. 138.) Simmons makes two mistakes here. First, his identification of the goods supplied by the law and due to which the duty to obey is supported by the fairness principle is not entirely correct. Second, his identification of the sense of dissatisfaction which would indicate that people don't prefer the law and obedience to no law and no obedience is also incorrect. It doesn't follow from the fact that people are unhappy with the taxes they pay, relative to the quality of the roads provided them, that they don't prefer the presence of law and obedience to their absence. The question is whether they are prepared to pay slightly unjust taxes in order that the legal system may exist as a mechanism for the institution and enforcement of desirable conducts.

[53] See also Greenawalt, *Conflicts of Law and Morality*, p. 142.

[54] For a similar position see G. Klosko, "The Principle of Fairness and Political Obligation," *Ethics* 97 (1986–7), 353. Klosko says that the principle of fairness applies to goods whose consumption cannot be avoided, if the existence of these goods is necessary for "a minimally acceptable life" (p. 355). Such goods must produce enjoyment. Rational people must desire them, be their other wishes what they may. The examples of such goods mentioned by Klosko are similar to those given in the text.

level. Most of us, I think, would view the preservation of a situation where the pollution level does not become deadly, as a necessary one from a moral point of view, regardless of whether people desire it in terms of their personal interests.[55] In order to prevent the pollution from reaching deadly levels, it is necessary for some, though not all, of the city's inhabitants to refrain from using their cars once a week. Fairness enters the picture at this point. Allowing some to use their cars while forbidding others to do so, would be unfair. Accordingly, everyone is obliged to refrain from using cars.

This matter is indicative of an important difference between the case of the entertainment center and that of the law. While most people have moral views according to which the existence of a legal system is necessary from a moral point of view,[56] they do not have moral views requiring the existence of entertainment centers. Thus, the combination of a morally necessary state of affairs, with considerations of fairness which enlarge the group of people required to bear the burdens needed for the maintenance of this state, applies in the case of the law, and doesn't apply in that of entertainment centers.

To sum up, the principle of fairness sets out to prevent the possibilities of free rides and exploitation. It has to do with states of affairs or institutions whose existence is supported even by those who consider shirking the burdens required by this existence, or should be supported by them, as their moral duty, despite the price of bearing the necessary burdens. The principle sets out to prevent people from shirking the burdens borne by others in order to maintain such states of affairs or institutions. It applies to two types of situations. In the first type, people desire the existence of a given situation, from the point of view of their personal interests and goals. If their preferences are such, then fairness requires that they share in the burdens necessary for its maintenance, even if it can be maintained without their participation. Most people want a legal system to exist. Thus, for most, the duty to obey the law can be derived, on this basis, from the principle of fairness. The second type of situation is such that it is

---

[55] On the assumption that some, and at least one, of the city's inhabitants wish(es) to go on living. If all of its inhabitants without exception prefer dying, I'm not convinced that we would still see the preservation of a state of affairs in which pollution does not become fatal, as morally mandatory.

[56] This majority also includes some of the writers against whom I'm arguing. For instance, Simmons, *Moral Principles and Political Obligations*, ch. 8, and also J. Raz, "Authority and Consent," *Virginia Law Review* 67 (1981), 103.

required by people's moral views. Many people hold that the existence of a legal system is mandatory from the moral point of view. For these, the principle of fairness is not only a basis for their own duty to obey the law. It is a basis for everyone's duty to obey the law.[57]

The principle of fairness, its limits, and the ways in which the duty to obey follows from it, may all be described in the following formalized manner. The problem addressed by the principle is: what are the requirements of fairness regarding the burdens involved in a production process necessitating the cooperation of many, the products of which are open to consumption not only by those whose participation was needed to produce these goods. Our subject is the requirements of fairness within the group of future consumers capable of producing. Several possible preferences exist within this group and with regard to the following packages:

Package A: The good without the burdens of its production (entertainment without payment, non-deadly air pollution without abstaining from use of cars, law without obedience);

Package B: The good along with the burdens of its production (entertainment and its payment, less-than-deadly air pollution and limited use of cars, law and obedience);

Package C: The absence of both the good and the burdens of its production (no entertainment and no payment, deadly air pollution and free use of cars, no law and no obedience);

Package D: The absence of the good in the presence of the burdens of its production (no entertainment though it is paid for, deadly air pollution and limited use of cars, obedience and an ineffective system of law).

The possible preferences are as follows: all members of the group

---

[57] As I shall show shortly, while discussing the argument from consequences, fairness doesn't require obedience to all laws on every occasion to which they apply. It requires that they be obeyed only when disobedience might cause damage or lead either directly or indirectly to negative consequences. The universality in question here is thus that of the duty to obey as regards its *subjects*, applying to all those subject to a legal system. It is not a universality as regards *acts* of obeying the law; it is not a duty to perform all acts of this kind. See also note 74, below.

prefer A to all the other packages; some members of the group prefer B to C (I'll call them the B–C group) and the rest prefer C to B (I'll call them the C–B group); all members of the group prefer any one of the packages A, B, C to package D.

It would seem that fairness requires all of the B–C group to choose B, whether the goods are only personally desirable (an entertainment center) or are required from the moral point of view (air with a less-than-deadly pollution level), as they also prefer A to B. This is so because although the good will be produced even if some of them choose A, it is impossible for all the members of the B–C group to choose A, and fairness requires equal treatment for those who share the same personal preferences. Those who prefer C to B, the members of the C–B group, cannot be made to share the burden, if the good in question is considered desirable from a personal point of view alone. This is because even if they find themselves with A in practice, and even if they are glad of it, forcing them to participate would mean forcing B rather than A upon them. Forcing B upon them would, in turn, be saddling them with a preference which they don't want, just because the B–C group has succeeded in realizing its preference. Forcing them to participate means forcing B–C upon them, despite the fact that they prefer C–B. This means unequal treatment of the members of the two groups, B–C and C–B.

However, when the good in question is one whose existence is considered necessary from the moral point of view, and when its production requires the cooperation of some of its future consumers, no one is allowed the actualization of preference C–B. (Let me emphasize, this is so from the viewpoint of whoever sees the good as morally mandatory.) Permitting C–B's realization means, by logical necessity, permitting the good's production to be foiled. Someone who prefers C–B and attempts to implement this preference is attempting an immoral act. All parties in the situation under discussion are barred from realizing the C–B preference, then. The only packages available in actuality are A and B. B is available to everyone, A to some only. However, according to our assumptions, everyone prefers A to B. Allowing some of those who want A to obtain it, while debarring others who want it from doing so, means allowing for the creation of inequality between equal personal wishes. As I have stated already with regard to the air pollution example, as A is obtainable for some only because some have shouldered B, allowing some the obtainment of A amounts to allowing those who get B to become a means of serving the personal wishes of those who get A, of allowing the former's parasitic exploitation by the latter. This would seem to be prohibited by morality. Again, it follows that someone who personally prefers the existence of law and obedience to it to no law and no obedience (and most people share this personal preference) is obliged by fairness to obey the law. For those who view the existence of a system of laws as morally mandatory (and most people, I believe, are of this opinion), everyone has a duty to obey the law, due to the requirements of fairness.

4. THE ARGUMENT FROM CONSEQUENCES

According to the argument presented and discussed below, the duty to obey the law follows directly from the negative consequences disobedience causes to society and to the quality of life within it. "Tell us, Socrates," Socrates says, speaking for the laws of Athens as they react to the possibility that he might disobey them and escape his death sentence, "what are you about? are you not going by an act of yours to overturn us – the laws, and the whole state, as far as in you lies? Do you imagine that a state can subsist and not be overthrown, in which the decisions of law have no power, but are set aside and trampled upon by individuals?"[58] Socrates, according to many, meant not only disobedience to court decisions, but disobedience to laws in general.

Two central points are made in criticism of the present argument. First, it is claimed that if indeed negative consequences might follow from acts which are cases of disobedience, it is usually superfluous to base a duty not to cause them on the fact that these are acts of disobedience.[59] Second, it is claimed that the present argument cannot justify the duty to perform all of the acts ordained by law. Though many acts of disobedience will lead to undesirable results, this is not true of all such acts. Accordingly, the argument from consequences can, at the very most, justify the duty to obey some, specific laws. It cannot support a general duty to obey the law *qua* law.[60]

[58] Plato, *Crito*, 50.
[59] Raz, *The Authority of Law*, pp. 245–9; "The Obligation to Obey: Revision and Tradition," *Notre Dame Journal of Law, Ethics and Public Policy* 1 (1984), 139, pp. 140–4.
[60] See Raz, *The Authority of Law*, p. 238; Smith, "Is There a *Prima Facie* Obligation to Obey the Law?," p. 965; A. D. Woozley, *Law and Obedience: The Arguments of Plato's Crito* (London: Duckworth, 1979), pp. 115–16.

I will examine two versions of the first claim, according to which the duty to obey the law is superfluous for the prevention of undesirable consequences following from acts of disobedience. One holds that the moral reasons supporting a form of conduct in keeping with the arrangements instituted by law draw their strength "from the factual existence of the social practice of cooperation [in the settled area] and not at all from the fact that the law is instrumental in its institution or its maintenance." Raz, whose claim this is,[61] illustrates the above by pointing out the practice of not polluting rivers. The answer to the moral question, whether or not to dump garbage into a river, depends, he claims, on the empirical question whether or not people are in the habit of refraining from it and not on the genesis of this practice. When the practice exists, then there are moral reasons for refraining from polluting, regardless of whether this practice originates in the law or elsewhere. When no such practice exists, and the river is constantly and heavily polluted, then the fact that a law forbids pollution doesn't alter the fact that there are no moral reasons for refraining from it.

This claim of Raz's would be totally correct if the goods produced by the legal system, the impairment of which is supposed to make the argument from consequences a basis for the duty to obey, were construed as the self-same goods created by the particular legal arrangements comprising the legal system (for instance: the goods produced by the laws that regulate matters of public security, or matters of education, health, town planning, etc.). These, however, are not the goods in view of whose possible impairment the argument from consequences becomes a basis for the duty to obey.[62] The good on whose account this duty follows from this argument is that of the existence of law as a tool for the institution and maintenance of various ordered forms of conduct. Raz himself says this of the law.[63] And the law's very existence as a tool of this type is a public good. The very existence of the institution of law is also the basis for the production of additional public goods, as its mere existence increases the degree of society's security and stability. Disobeying any law, *qua* law, may damage these goods, in various manners described below

---

[61] See Raz, *The Authority of Law*, p. 249.
[62] Here, Greenawalt also makes a mistake similar to Raz's. See his *Conflicts of Law and Morality*, p. 104. However, it should be noted that in speaking of the argument from fairness, Greenawalt is aware of the possibility of construing it as applying to the law on different levels. *Ibid.*, pp. 136–8.   [63] *Ibid.*, for example, pp. 246–7.

(just as interfering with the practice of refraining from a river's pollution may damage the public good consisting of the pollution-free river). I accept, then, that regarding the creation of a particular good produced by a practice that is instituted by a particular legal regulation, the question whether or not to adhere to this practice is answered in terms of whether or not the practice itself is adhered to, and not in terms of the origins, i.e. legal or other, of this practice. All of this, though, has no bearing whatsoever upon the question whether or not one must adhere to the practice in question because the law ordains it. The answer to this question should be given with regard to the goods produced by the legal system as such, and not with regard to the particular good produced by the practice of a particular legal rule.

At this point though it is pertinent to recourse to, and elaborate slightly upon, the familiar jurisprudential distinction between actions which are inherently bad (*mala per se*) and those which are bad because they are prohibited (*mala prohibita*). Assault is an example of the former. In order that assaults be considered wrong, there is no need for their prohibition to be practiced, and there is certainly no need for it to be practiced as a legal prohibition. Failure to pay taxes is an example of an action in which there is no wrong unless its prohibition is practiced, as taxpaying is intended to create the good consisting of the existence of a public budget, and it is only when a certain number of people (just how many depending on the nature of the tasks the budget undertakes) pay their taxes regularly, that this good has a chance of being created. If the prohibition is not practiced, the good will not be created and thus there is no wrong in failure to pay taxes.

However, in view of the above, if a legal prohibition is practiced as regards taxpaying, then this makes failure to pay wrong in two courts from which it would have not looked wrong had this prohibition been absent. One of these is the danger caused by disobeying the prohibition, to creation of the good arising from this specific prohibition, the good consisting of the existence of a public budget. The second is the danger caused by disobeying the prohibition, to the creation of goods achieved by the legal system as such: the good consisting of the existence of an institution through which it is possible to determine publicly and clearly, and to enforce, modes of conduct that are considered desirable of themselves or that will become desirable upon becoming general practices, and the good consisting in the existence of the possibility of enhancing the levels of security, stability and certainty as to people's conduct in society. (These are second-order goods; goods for the creation of goods.)

It is worth noting that some actions are *mala per se*, but become *mala prohibita* as well when prohibited by law, both in the first and second senses distinguished above. If a legal rule creates or supports the practice of refraining from assault, then what departure from this practice means is not only damage to the victim, but also damage to society members' sense of personal safety and damage to the law's operation as a tool for determining and enforcing conducts. I shall reiterate what has been said here in the table below.

It is worth noting that the two types of *mala prohibita* differ in an important way. While the enactment of a legal prohibition may constitute a condition for the *prevention* of the wrongs denoted by the first type, it is the very *creation* of the wrongs denoted by the second type for which such enactment forms a necessary condition. The first type of *mala prohibita* denotes a wrong that exists independently of the legal instruction, which is nonetheless a major way of preventing it. The wrong of the absence of a public budget is a difficult one to prevent when the duty to pay taxes isn't imposed by law. Conversely, the second type of *mala prohibita* denotes a wrong that could not occur in the absence of the prohibition. The legal rule, in this case, is a necessary condition for the very possibility of the wrong's occurrence, and not a means of preventing a wrong that will occur in case the rule isn't enacted and practiced. The goods created through the existence of the legal system, the good of the very existence of this system as a tool for determining and enforcing desirable conducts, and the possibilities of security, stability and certainty that lie in its correct operation, could not be damaged in any way through people's failure to pay taxes, were there no law commanding people to do so.

The table illustrates that it is only the negative consequences of the third type, and the threat of their occurrence, due to which the argument from consequences can serve to support the duty to obey the law. It also illustrates that this argument can serve as grounds for the duty to perform actions commanded by many laws in more than one way and without the mediation of the duty to obey the law.

The following should however be kept in mind: if refraining from the actions ordained by the law may damage the goods created by the legal system as such, that is, the goods positioned at the bottom of the table above, then the argument from consequences justifies a duty to

	Disobedience to a law prohibiting assault	Disobedience to a law imposing taxpaying
Mala per se	Damage to the victim	—
Mala prohibita A	Damage to the sense of personal security within the group in general	Damage to the good consisting in the existence of a public budget
Mala prohibita B	Damage to the law's operation as a tool for determining and enforcing desirable conducts in the first two senses, and damage to the other goods created by the law: the sense of society's security, certainty and stability	

perform these actions due to the fact of their being ordained by legal regulations. It justifies a duty to obey the law. It does so independently of and in addition to any other duties which it may justify with regard to the performance of these actions.

The second version of the criticism presenting the duty to obey the law as superfluous points out that this duty, even if it did exist, would suffer from chronic unemployment. Actions required by good laws are not in need of its aid, as these laws should be obeyed for the same reasons that make them good laws and not because of the negative consequences caused by disobedience to the legal system as a whole.[64] On this version, the duty to obey the law would only serve to urge obedience to bad laws. However, this duty is usually overridden in the case of morally bad laws.[65] It thus turns out that in the only cases where the duty to obey could actually be of practical use, it is not available for such use. However, this line of criticism also fails. Legal systems that are morally sound and that are, indeed, the only kind of systems to which the duty to obey applies,[66] may include many laws that are not morally bad but are nonetheless inadequate in some other sense. For instance, tax laws might be considered (and also actually be) bad from the point of view of economic efficiency. Planning laws might be considered bad from an aesthetic point of view. Arms policies might be strategically bad, etc. Such laws supply the duty to obey with more than enough work. This is so as, on the

[64] For example, Smith, "Is There a *Prima Facie* Obligation to Obey the Law?," pp. 969–73, and Raz, "The Obligation to Obey: Revision and Tradition," p. 140.

[65] For an extensive discussion of this point see chapter 4, pp. 121–7, below.

[66] On this point too see chapter 3, below.

assumption that they are bad, breaking them would not necessarily lead to bad results in terms of the particular goods that they supposedly produce. The only reason left for obeying such laws would accordingly be the need to protect the good that is protected by the duty to obey the law, i.e. the law's existence as an institution determining forms of conduct of and within the community, along with the levels of security, stability and certainty ensured by this institution. Nevertheless, it is true that with regard to most of the actions required by laws, it is not because of the duty to obey that people should perform these actions. This, however, comes as no surprise. All of us know that the duty to obey the law usually serves to urge and justify the performance of actions when the issue is obedience to defective laws.

The second line of criticism of the argument from consequences indicates what I consider to be the correct fact, that not all cases of disobedience to laws have negative consequences. The critical anarchists conclude that, in view of this, the argument from consequences cannot serve as a basis for the duty to obey the law. This conclusion is reached via the following route: the duty to obey the law is a duty to perform acts simply because they are required by the law. However, the argument from consequences doesn't justify the performance of each and every act of obeying the law. It follows from this that it doesn't justify a general duty to obey the law as law. Ergo, it does not supply a basis for the duty to obey the law.

The factual claim on which this line of criticism is based is indeed correct.[67] Disobedience to laws may indeed endanger and damage the law's operation as a tool for determining and enforcing desirable forms of conduct. It may do so in various ways and directions. And yet, not all cases of disobedience involve risks or damage of this type. Disobedience may damage the law's function as a tool for determining and enforcing conduct, directly. Very few cases of disobedience present this type of risk, though. It is only when the functioning of the legal system is very poor that individual cases of disobedience may cause it direct damage. (Needless to say, I'm referring to disobedience on the part of subjects. Disobedience on the part of the authorities whose role it is to enforce the law is far more dangerous in the present sense. On this issue, see also chapter 4.) The main danger to the law's

---

[67] For an opposite stance on this point see John Finnis, "The Authority of Law in the Predicament of Contemporary Social Theory," *Notre Dame Journal of Law, Ethics and Public Policy* 1 (1984), 115.

operation implicit in subjects' disobedience is an indirect one. Disobedience may encourage additional cases of disobedience, thus causing the deterioration of its operation as a tool for determining and enforcing desirable conduct. Here too, though, the danger is not universal.

There are two reasons due to which disobedience may encourage additional cases of disobedience. First, it may undermine the expectations of witnesses that the law will indeed function as a tool of the type described. What point is there in refraining from disobeying the law due to the duty to obey it, if it doesn't succeed in functioning as such a tool in any case? The second reason why disobedience may encourage more disobedience is a far graver and weightier one than the first, and has to do with the matter of fairness. The law's operation as a tool for determining and enforcing conduct doesn't necessarily depend, as we have already seen, upon obedience on the part of each and every potential beneficiary of this function. However, the principle of fairness, as we have also already seen, requires the obedience of all beneficiaries. Disobedience, if it can't be allowed equally, undermines the fairness of the distribution of goods and burdens, and thus means the exploitation of those who obey. This argument clearly plays an important part in people's moral psychology, including the psychology active in the context of the present discussion. One of the ways in which the obedient may prevent their exploitation, and restore equality with the disobedient, is to disobey. In other words, disobedience may engender more disobedience not only because it may arouse its witnesses' doubts as to the production of the good which obedience is supposed to produce, but also because of such witnesses' justified wishes not to be exploited.

In saying these wishes are justified, I do not mean to say that it is justified to act upon them all things considered. Much may be said about the conditions that must be met in order for it to be decisively justified to act on such a wish, but I cannot undertake to discuss this issue here. In the present context, what is important is the causal force of the principle of fairness in the psychology of human action. Here, it must be noted that justified wishes, even if it isn't justified to act upon them, have greater motivating force than wishes which are totally unjustified. If disobeying the law on the part of some of its subjects is unfair to those who obey it, then this gives the latter reason to disobey it themselves. Even though this reason may only rarely, or never, be reason enough for disobedience, it still has significant causal motivating force. This is doubly so in the circumstances presently under discussion, circumstances in which the temptation to disobey is great, and in view of most people's tendency to "concoct" their moral thought to suit their private interests, and their tendency to adorn their private interests in moral attire.

Individual cases of disobedience thus endanger the good's production by encouraging additional cases of disobedience for reasons having to do with fairness. This danger is a real one. Nevertheless, it too is not universal.[68] There may be circumstances such that universal disobedience to the laws applying to them would cause no negative consequences, either direct or indirect, to the good in whose name the argument from consequences is offered as a basis for the duty to obey. When laws apply to circumstances of this kind, the duty to obey them cannot be based either upon the argument from consequences or the principle of fairness. As what is under discussion is disobedience that has no negative consequences, the argument from consequences simply doesn't apply. As it is also a case of disobedience in which no damage will be caused even if everyone disobeys, the principle of fairness doesn't apply either. Exemption from the burden of obedience may be distributed equally here; it can include everyone. A trivial example of such a possibility is disobeying the law prohibiting one to cross the street while the stoplight is red, at 3 a.m., with no one there to see.[69] Such a crossing does no direct or indirect damage (not only to the good in whose name the argument from consequences is offered as a basis for the duty to obey, but also to the other goods in whose name this argument is supposed to necessitate

---

[68] One point emphasized by the last claim should be repeated: it cites the argument from consequences, and not the fairness principle, as requiring obedience on a large scale. It requires this due to fairness. This should not be confused with two other theses. First, it should not be confused with the thesis according to which considerations of fairness may be based on considerations of utility. (On the attempts to base fairness on utility and their failure, see David Lyons, *Forms and Limits of Utilitarianism* [Oxford: Oxford University Press, 1965], pp. 172–7.) It is precisely because fairness has an independent moral status, or at least because people view fairness as having such status and do not wish to be exploited, that an unfair action is not only unfair, but also causes undesirable consequences. Second, it should not be confused with the thesis that the principle of fairness requires obedience on a large scale itself, not only as an aid to the argument from consequences. The effect of the principle of fairness is thus twofold: it directly requires obedience on the part of all of the goods' consumers even when this obedience isn't immediately necessary for the goods' production, and it is central to the argument from negative consequences which requires obedience even when it isn't immediately necessary for the goods' production.

[69] See also Greenawalt, *Conflicts of Law and Morality*, pp. 179–80.

obedience to stoplights). Refraining from such a crossing is a burden
that everyone can be exempted from, a burden the exemption from
which can be distributed equally.

Thus, the thesis according to which the argument from consequences (and the fairness argument) does not support obedience to
all laws in all the circumstances to which they apply is a correct one.
(As we shall see later, this is also true of the two bases for the duty to
obey discussed forthwith, the one anchored in the duty to support just
institutions and the other anchored in communal obligations.) This
means that the duty to obey the law is not universal with regard to
the act-tokens falling under it. At times its justifications fail to apply
at all, or to require certain actions demanded by the law.

However, does this truth entail the conclusion contended by
critical anarchism, that is, that there is no duty to obey the law? The
idea that it does is apparently motivated by another truth regarding
the duty to obey (and other generic duties such as keeping promises
or refraining from homicide), a truth to which I have already had
recourse in the first chapter.[70] If a duty to obey the law or to keep
promises indeed exists, then particular actions falling within these
act-types become duties by virtue of belonging to these types. For
instance, actions are duties under the duty to keep promises, by virtue
of having been promised, and not due to any other of their qualities.
Similarly, an action ordained by law is a duty because it is ordained
by law, and not due to any other quality it may possess. If this is so,
however, how is it possible that there are acts required by the law that
are nonetheless not duties, i.e. are not required by the reasons
justifying obedience to the law? Indeed, there would seem to be no
such duty.

The first point to be noticed here is that the present move, if made
with regard to the duty to obey the law, should also be made with
regard to duties such as keeping promises and the prohibition of
homicide. It may easily be shown that the justifications offered by
philosophers for these duties do not apply to each of the individual
act-tokens falling under them. It follows, by the logic guiding the
present anarchist critique of the duty to obey, that there is in fact no
duty to keep promises or refrain from homicide. As regards the duty
not to commit homicide, philosophers have claimed, and to my mind
convincingly so, that it is based on two important justifications. First,
on the value of the lives of those creatures which are capable of

[70] See pp. 14–17 above.

happiness and enjoyment. Second, on the unique value of the lives of creatures capable of consciousness, rationality and autonomy. However, there are clearly humans who are incapable of either enjoyment or autonomy. One valid conclusion following from this is that with regard to some, specific human beings, the justifications for prohibiting homicide do not apply. The arguments in favor of euthanasia and abortion are based, at least in part, on this conclusion and on the line of thought leading up to it.[71] In other words, the duty not to kill is not universal in the same sense that the duty to obey the law is not universal. Similar things may be said of the duty to keep promises.

However, do we wish to continue from here, from the fact that these two duties are not universal, to the conclusion that we are not duty-bound to keep promises or to refrain from homicide? This seems a somewhat exorbitant price to pay. In fact, it is even higher than it seems. It would seem, in point of fact, that we would have to give up almost all of the duties possessed of any reasonable degree of specificity.[72] Is there, however, any way of avoiding such a conclusion?

An affirmative answer to the present question depends upon a more thorough clarification of the relation between the fact of an action's being of a certain type, and the fact of its becoming a duty. As stated, what this relation means is that particular actions, rendered duties under an act-type, are thus rendered because they are of this type, and not due to any other features they may possess. But the relation in question also means that the particular actions becoming duties under a certain act-type become so non-contingently. They are rendered duties due to a non-contingent characteristic of the type.

It is easy to find many examples where the fact that the law requires an act is a reason to perform it. A person may be expelled from school or lose his job if rumors that he broke the law become known to his headmaster or employer. His criminal act(s) may greatly aggrieve his much-loved parents or spouse, etc. Such considerations do not even tend to show that there is an obligation to obey the law. For although in these cases the law (i.e. the fact

---

[71] See e.g. Jonathan Glover, *Causing Death and Saving Lives* (Harmondsworth: Penguin, 1977), chs. 9–11, 15; Peter Singer, *Practical Ethics* (Cambridge: Cambridge University Press, 1979), chs. 6–7.

[72] Apparently, the only duties with which we will be left will be those formulated in terms of the most abstract and fundamental moral principles (such as the principle of utility, for instance, or that of the categorical imperative).

that the law requires an action) is a reason for conforming behavior it is an incidental reason existing for a particular person, applying under certain special circumstances.

Raz, the source of this quotation, sums it up by saying, "The obligation to obey the law is a general obligation applying to all the law's subjects and to all the laws on all the occasions to which they apply."[73]

This summarizing thesis that the duty to obey must be universal is put forward as if it were equivalent to, or at least entailed by, the thesis preceding it. According to the former thesis, when the performance of a given action is a duty under the duty to obey the law this means that its performance is a duty on the basis of reasons related non-contingently to the law. However, does the thesis of universality indeed follow from the thesis of non-contingency? The same question must be asked of the other duties mentioned above, and the answer depends upon the explication appropriate to the thesis of non-contingency.

Indeed, it may be construed at various levels of strictness. The feature or features making the given act-type (obeying the law, keeping promises, refraining from homicide) a duty may be considered to be necessary to the type in question. However, a lesser degree of severity is also maintainable. It may be claimed that the said features are typical of, rather than necessary to, these types of actions. It is, for example, typical of homicide that it involves the annihilation of creatures capable of enjoyment and/or desires and/or autonomy, but it is not necessary that this be the case. (For instance, the killing of creatures biologically classifiable as humans, who have suffered an irreversible loss of consciousness, is not an annihilation of creatures capable of enjoyment and/or desires and/or autonomy.) It is typical of breaking promises that it is an action weakening an institution intended to serve interpersonal reliances in society. This is not a necessary feature, however. (For instance: breaking trivial promises of which the promisees have forgotten, and of which no third party is aware, will not weaken the social system of interpersonal reliances.) It is typical of the act-type of disobeying the law that it endangers an institution intended to serve society's stability, security, order and coordination. Again, though, this is not a necessity. (For example: driving through an intersection on a red light, at 2 a.m.,

[73] Raz, *The Authority of Law*, p. 234; see also Soper, "The Obligation to Obey the Law," pp. 128, 132.

when there are no witnesses, will not undermine this institution and will not endanger the stability, security, order or coordination of society.)

To reiterate, the position being examined here is the one according to which generic duties are universal in the sense that each particular act falling under them is supported by the reasons due to which the generic duty is indeed a duty. Only those who adopt the stricter conception of the non-contingency requirement described above, viewing it as necessity, are bound to this position. The less strict conception, according to which non-contingency means typicality, does not entail the requirement of universality.

It is difficult to point out convincing reasons for adopting the strict conception. Consider the question: is there a necessary feature of law due to which the actions it requires become moral duties? Is there a necessary feature of human beings due to which killing them is impermissible? It would seem unnecessary to answer these in the affirmative, in order to maintain that the duty to obey the law is a duty to perform acts because they are ordered by law, and that the duty to avoid homicide is a duty not to kill creatures because they are human. It seems quite sufficient to give affirmative answers to the more modest versions of these questions: is there anything typical of law which makes acts required by laws into duties? Is there anything typical of killing humans due to which acts belonging to this type are impermissible? As stated, making do with this more modest reading of non-contingency will prevent commitment to the universality of the duties in question. According to this conception, the duty to obey the law is indeed a duty to perform actions on the basis of non-contingent features of the institution of law, but this does not entail that every action required by the law is supported by the reasons that justify the duty to obey. Similarly, the duty to keep promises is indeed a duty to perform actions on the basis of non-contingent features of the institution of promising, but this does not entail that all promised actions are supported by the reasons which justify the duty to keep promises.

I have hopefully shown it possible to understand the relation between the fact that an act is required by law and the fact it becomes a duty, in a manner that does not entail the universal presence of the reasons justifying the generic duty, in every instance involving particular actions falling under it. If I am right, then the bad consequences of very many instances of disobedience, relating to the value that we ascribe to the existence of this institution, support a duty to obey the law. This duty, though, is not universal in the sense discussed here.[74] This is also true of the argument based on the principle of fairness, as well as the argument discussed forthwith, namely the one that is linked with the duty to support just institutions.

5. THE DUTY TO SUPPORT JUST INSTITUTIONS

In *A Theory of Justice*, John Rawls suggests that the duty to obey the law be based on the "natural duty to justice." This latter comprises two parts: "first, we are to comply with and to do our share in just institutions when they exist and apply to us; and second, we are to assist in the establishment of just arrangements when they do not exist, at least when this can be done with little cost to ourselves."[75] The antecedent of the first part of this duty to justice can serve, according to Rawls, as a basis of the duty to obey.

This basis has been questioned and criticized, in view of the question: when will institutions count as "applying to us"? If the answer to this question stems from the decisions of the just institution itself, it is not at all clear that we will indeed wish to say that we have a duty to obey its orders. Saying this would mean saying that any institution is entitled to force itself upon us, on the sole condition that it be just. On the other hand, if the answer depends upon our decisions, this means that we have consented to the institution. Consequently, we are duty-bound to obey by virtue of this consent. But as we have shown above, it can't be said of many of us that we have given our consent as regards this matter.[76] It accordingly seems that the present attempt to base the duty to obey the law will meet, at the hands of the critics, a fate similar to that met by the attempt to

---

[74] However, it is universal as regards its subjects, in the sense that it applies to all people. Perhaps it is worth noting here further that the duty to obey is not universal as regards the actions to which it applies, in a manner that differs from the non-universality of rules such as "It is generally desirable to take two vacations a year." Rules of this type are not universal in the sense that no harm is done when someone who usually abides by them departs from them from time to time. The exceptions to these rules are justified in reference to the relevant biography of their violators. The non-universality of the duty to obey the law, the duty not to kill and the duty to keep promises is of a different kind. When the reasons that justify these generic duties apply to particular actions belonging to them, those to whom the duties apply must perform these actions, regardless of their personal record of abiding by them up until that moment. These duties are thus non-universal in the sense that the reasons supporting them do not apply at times. When they do apply though, they necessarily create duties, and for all people.   [75] Rawls, *A Theory of Justice*, p. 334.

[76] For this line of criticism see Simmons, *Moral Principles and Political Obligations*, pp. 147–52.

offer the principle of fairness as a basis. It will either collapse of its own accord or it will merge with the argument from consent and collapse along with it.

One way of saving Rawls' argument from criticism of this kind is interpreting the phrase "applying to us" as one which is neither addressed to the institutions' own decisions or to the decisions of those supposedly duty-bound to obey them. A third interpretation is possible. Such an interpretation is implicit in the attempt made by Dworkin, and discussed in the next section, to base the duty to obey on communal obligation.[77] In speaking of these communal obligations, Dworkin speaks of the fact that people's membership in a community is determined by criteria based on social practice, not on the community's formal decision and not even, necessarily, on the individual's voluntary choice. "Most people think," he says, "that they have associative obligations just by belonging to groups defined by social practice, which is not necessarily a matter of choice or consent…"[78] Social ties such as friendships, and biological ties such as family relations, are examples of ties that create such duties, ties which are not dependent upon choice or consent.

As we shall see shortly, Dworkin fails to clarify the contents of communal obligations; i.e. the exact actions required under them. The duty of supporting just institutions and communal obligation may thus complement each other. Communal obligations can serve as a key to the identification of those subject to the duty of supporting just institutions. They may consequently offer a source in the light of which the phrase "applying to us" can be understood in the context of the latter duty. The duty of supporting just institutions can, on the other hand, offer a key to the identification of at least some of the contents of communal obligations. It can provide a source allowing for recognizing the actions which these commit us to perform. I shall elaborate further on this last point in my discussion of communal obligations. At the moment though, it is the first point that should be stressed: the social customs defining groups within which communal obligations are created may provide a meaning for the phrase "applying to us" in the framework of the duty to support just institutions. In this manner, they may free Rawls' attempt to base the duty to obey the law on the latter duty from the present criticism of it.

[77] See the following section of this chapter, pp. 83–9.
[78] Dworkin, *Law's Empire*, pp. 195–6.

In any case, John Simmons, whose criticism of Rawls is of the type described, tries other rescue routes. He asks whether this may be accomplished by dropping the "applying to us" condition altogether from the definition of the duty to support just institutions.[79] Such an omission would mean that we have a duty to support just institutions wherever they are. Simmons believes that this should be rejected as a basis for the duty to obey, as it saddles people with an impractically heavy load.

This point, rather than serving as a justification for rejecting the duty to support just institutions as a basis for the duty to obey serves as a justification for limiting this duty. The limitations can take on two forms. First, the duty may be limited so as to apply to only some just institutions – to those whose existence we consider morally necessary (in the sense assigned this concept above, throughout my discussion of the argument from fairness). Second, the duty to obey just institutions may be limited so as to require refrainment from harming these institutions, rather than acting positively to support them. Both strategies will decrease the load involved in the duty to obey just institutions. Nonetheless, the duty in question will also continue to support the duty to obey, as the law is an institution thought by many to be morally mandatory, and, as shown by the argument from consequences, the duty to obey it is a duty to refrain from endangering or damaging it.[80]

One last remark regarding this last point: the derivation of the duty to obey the law from the duty to support just institutions is based on a factual assumption identical to the one that served the derivation from the argument from consequences. The duty to support just institutions may only be translated into a duty to obey the law due to the fact that disobedience may cause undesirable consequences for the institution of law. As stated, according to the argument from consequences, this is just the reason why we shouldn't disobey the law. The two arguments also share similar ranges of application. First, the argument from consequences doesn't apply to unjust institutions. Though this is not explicitly stated by its premises, as it is by the premises of the argument from the duty to support just institutions, it is nonetheless anchored in its presuppositions, as we shall see in the course of the next two chapters. Second, the duty to support just institutions, in serving as basis for the duty to obey,

---

[79] Simmons, *Moral Principles and Political Obligations*, p. 153.
[80] See also Greenawalt, *Conflicts of Law and Morality*, p. 167.

doesn't engender a universal duty to obey. Neither, as we have seen, does the argument from consequences. This is because refraining from disobedience that doesn't endanger the law doesn't mean supporting the institution of law. Thus, from the point of view of the duty to support just institutions, it is not our duty to refrain from such disobedience. The duty to obey supported by this argument is accordingly not universal. It does not, however, follow that the two arguments are identical despite their common factual premise and identical ranges of application. Their major premises are not identical. What the one relies upon is that we shouldn't perform acts with potentially bad consequences. What the other relies on is our duty to support just institutions.[81]

An additional objection has been advanced against the attempt to ground the duty to obey in the duty to support just institutions. Such a basis, it has been claimed, and this actually applies to the argument from consequences as well, fails to capture the unique intimacy characteristic of the relationship between citizen and country. "That duty [to support just institutions]...," says Dworkin, "does not provide a good explanation of legitimacy, because it does not tie political obligation sufficiently tightly to the particular community to which those who have the obligation belong; it does not show why Britons have any special duty to support the institutions of Britain."[82] Simmons voices similar remarks.[83]

If we choose to construe the duty to support just institutions as one which holds only for the institutions "applying to us," while assigning this concept the reading described above, that is, in keeping with the customs defining those groups within which we have communal obligations, then the attempt to base the duty to obey on the duty to

---

[81] It would also seem that the attempt to base the duty to obey the law on the duty to support just institutions is more suited to deontological moral theories, while the attempt to base it on the negative consequences of disobedience is more suited to consequentialist theories. However, it would be incorrect to believe, as Greenawalt seems to, that the argument from consequences is uniquely consequentialist. The duty not to cause negative consequences may form a component of a deontological ethics. Ross, in *The Right and The Good*, indeed, cites a similar duty, the duty to produce as much good as possible, as one of the duties comprising his deontology and furthermore sees this duty as one of the bases of the duty to obey the law ("the duty of obeying the laws of one's country arises partly...from the fact that its laws are potent instruments for the general good," *ibid.*, pp. 27–8). As basing the duty to obey the law on the argument from consequences is not unique to consequentialist theories of morality, I saw no need to tire the reader with the intricacies of the distinctions between consequentialism and deontology as regards the duty to obey.

[82] See Dworkin, *Law's Empire*, p. 193.

[83] Simmons, *Moral Principles and Political Obligations*, pp. 155–6.

support just institutions is clearly immune to the present line of criticism. However, such criticism must also be disproved by any who conceive of the duty to support just institutions as a duty to all just institutions, rather than only to those "applying to us" specifically. It must be disproved as it presupposes a much too rigid understanding of the intimacy relation between a citizen and his or her community in the context of the duty to obey the law.

As proposed in the first chapter, the duty to obey the law is, first and foremost, a person's duty to his or her community. It is, however, more than this. When visiting other countries, we also have a duty to obey their laws.[84] The duty to support just institutions may supply one of the explanations for this fact.[85] Another explanation may be provided by the argument from consequences.

Pragmatic considerations may clarify how these arguments apply mainly to the laws of the community of which one is a member, though in principle they require observation of the laws of all countries. People have more chances of supporting the law of the country in which they live than they do of supporting those of other countries. Most of the opportunities for disobedience and causing bad consequences arise within the community of which people are members. Both Dworkin and Simmons mention these pragmatic considerations, but see their incorporation as missing the unique intimacy between citizen and country, an intimacy that forms the basis of political obligation. Even if Dworkin and Simmons are right, and these pragmatic considerations fail to provide an exhaustive explanation for one's special duty to obey the law of one's community, this is no reason to totally disqualify the duty to support just institutions in its present reading, or the argument from consequences, as grounds for the duty to obey the law. What it indicates is

[84] Naturally, if states of which we are not citizens make unjustifiable demands upon us, for instance that we serve in their armies, then the duty to obey their laws or their unjustified laws is void or canceled. However, this is also true, as we shall see, of the unjustifiable demands of the states in which we do live. These too, as we shall see in the next two chapters, are rendered void at times or are overridden due to their unjustifiability. Moreover, the fact that some demands are justified when made by the states of which we are citizens and unjustified when made by states of which we are not, is one that makes the scope of the obedience owed by us to the state of which we are citizens much larger than that owed by us to other states. However, this doesn't result from the fact that the duty to obey is limited to the relations between citizens and their countries, but rather from the many limitations applying to what other states are entitled to demand of us, relative to what our state may demand.

[85] See also Greenawalt, *Conflicts of Law and Morality*, p. 167. Other explanations may be given for the duty to obey the laws of other countries, for instance, avoiding ingratitude towards our hosts.

merely that if these were the only grounds of this duty, we would lack a full explanation for the fact that the duty to obey is mainly a citizen's duty to his or her own country. However, the duty to obey has additional grounds. These, in turn, provide for full clarification of the fact in question.

One of these bases, already discussed above, is that of the principle of fairness. This basis relates to the benefits one gains from the institution of law. These benefits are, for the most part, produced by the law of one's country. It is consequently mainly to one's fellow community members, whose obedience facilitates the existence of this law, that the duty to obey is addressed. This explanation of why the duty to obey is mainly one's duty to the law of one's country goes deeper than the pragmatic one which accompanied the former arguments. And yet, the most thoroughgoing explanation for this point is undoubtedly supplied by the attempt to base the duty to obey which I have already had recourse to and will now proceed to discuss separately in detail, that is, Dworkin's attempt to base it on communal obligation.

6. COMMUNAL OBLIGATION

Dworkin suggests that the duty to obey be viewed as a member of the class of duties which he calls associative or communal. Typical examples of these duties pertain to family and friends. The source of such duties cannot be anchored in the free choice of their subjects. "Even associations we consider mainly consensual, like friendship, are not formed in one act of deliberate contractual commitment, the way one joins a club..."[86] And if the duty of friendship is difficult to explain on grounds of choice and consent, then it is most certainly difficult to recourse to such a basis in the case of family and other obligations.

People have such duties by virtue of their membership in groups, even if they haven't chosen or consented to belong to these groups. They are duties one has by virtue of one's membership in natural or emergent groups. Membership in such groups is considered grounds for the duties in question, due to social practice. Political obligation, Dworkin claims, can be seen as one of the communal obligations. "Common assumptions... about associative responsibilities suggest that political obligation might be counted among them..."[87] Later, he attempts to uphold and enhance the last thesis.

[86] Dworkin, *Law's Empire*, p. 197.   [87] *Ibid.*, pp. 195–6.

There are three theses that should be distinguished in Dworkin's discussion. According to the first, communal obligations are *a possible basis for political obligation*. According to the second, they are *the only possible basis for this obligation*. According to the third, communal obligations are *the basis for the duty to obey the law*.

It seems to me that Dworkin succeeds in substantiating only the first thesis. He does so by rejecting the reasons that he sees as having motivated philosophers to overlook the possibility that communal obligations might be the source of political obligation. There are two such reasons. One is the view that communal obligations assume the existence of emotional ties between the obliged party and the party to whom the obligation is owed. Ties of this type presuppose personal acquaintance, which does not exist in most cases between the members of a political community as such. Dworkin rejects this reason in the belief that emotional ties are not a necessary condition for the development of duties of communal membership. He believes that these duties presuppose the existence of specific attitudes on the part of those affiliated with them. The affiliated parties are obliged to conceive of them as special duties that they have to each other, duties that they don't have to those outside of the relationship. They must conceive of them as personal duties; the members of the group in which such duties develop owe them to each other personally, and not to the group collectively. They "must see these responsibilities as flowing from a more general responsibility each has of *concern* for the well being of others in the group," and they "must suppose that the group's practices show not only concern but an equal concern for all members."[88] However, Dworkin believes that these conditions for the existence of a communal obligation are not psychological ones. They are, rather, conditions in the light of which responsibility is determined within the group. "Though a group will rarely meet or long sustain them unless its members by and large feel some emotional bond with one another, the conditions do not themselves demand this."[89] The first reason, then, that Dworkin sees as motivating philosophers to neglect the possibility of viewing political obligation as a communal obligation is not a valid one. It is not the case that the existence of communal obligations necessarily presupposes the existence of love or even personal acquaintance between those whose duties to each other these are.

The second reason why philosophers neglect the possibility of

---

[88] *Ibid.*, pp. 199–200.   [89] *Ibid.*, p. 201.

basing political obligation on communal membership is that such a stance carries an aura of nationalism or even racism. This reason too is rejected by Dworkin. Communal obligations are a legitimate subject for critical interpretation, at the core of which are the values of justice and fairness. Such interpretation can fend off the threats of militant nationalism and racism posed by the duties of communal membership, in several ways. It can indicate the voidness of specific communal obligations due to their injustice. It can prescribe a skeptical and dismissive attitude towards entire systems of customs of communal obligations, when these are fundamentally or completely tainted with injustice. It can point out the existence of a real dilemma where communal obligation clashes with the duties of justice, when one of the obligations overrides the other. In other words, according to Dworkin, even if communal obligations can bear grave dangers of militant nationalism, they are limited by the requirements of justice. In order to contain the threats of militant nationalism, it is thus not necessary to give up, completely, "the more wholesome ideals of national community and the special responsibility these support."[90]

This seems to me to be correct. The last argument is consistent with the meaning of the concept of duty as defined in the first chapter, and with the conditions and limits of the duty to obey to be discussed in the following chapters. Perhaps Dworkin underemphasizes the fact that communal obligations endanger the values of justice to a greater degree than duties generated themselves by the value of justice. (Such dangers, by the way, are not only imminent in the political communal obligation. The communal obligations of family and friendship also bear these dangers.) However, he is correct in maintaining that the fact that they pose such risks is not reason enough for giving them up or banishing them from our moral world. It is only reason enough for being extremely watchful here, for employing the utmost caution to prevent these dangers from becoming actualities. The mechanism recommended by Dworkin for channeling and implementing this caution – a skeptical attitude towards systems which have already contracted these dangers, or the possibility of preferring the duties of justice to those of communality – seems quite sufficient.

Dworkin's argument against the thesis that communal obligations necessarily assume the existence of emotional interpersonal ties involving personal acquaintance is also one that seems convincing. A detailed discussion of it would require a careful analysis of communal

---

[90] *Ibid.*, pp. 202–6.

obligations, an analysis which would exceed the scope of my discussion. I would like to say, though, that even if it turned out that Dworkin had employed insufficient means for showing personal acquaintance to be unnecessary for a communal obligation, he would still be able to recourse to an additional justification for his thesis. Personal acquaintances are not a necessary condition for the generation of communal obligations, as people also develop feelings of care and worry towards those whom they don't know personally. They develop such sentiments towards those who are culturally and historically close to themselves, or those who share their origins or fates, even without having met them. It accordingly seems that emotional ties stemming from personal acquaintance are not a necessary condition for the creation of communal obligations.

All of this, however, only supports Dworkin's first thesis, i.e. that communal obligations are a possible basis for the duties one has to the political community of which one is a member. They don't suffice to substantiate his second thesis, that they are the only possible basis for this duty, or his third thesis, that communal obligations are a basis for the duty to obey the law.

The thesis of the exclusivity of communal obligations as a foundation for political obligation is anchored in the rejection of some of the other foundations offered for this obligation. Dworkin rejects attempts to ground the duty to obey on fairness, consent and the duty to support just institutions. I have already rejected his criticism of the last, above. His criticism on the other two arguments is similar to that offered by other theoreticians and discussed in the previous sections. If my conclusions on these two arguments are correct, then both the argument from fairness and the argument from negative consequences, ignored by Dworkin, survive the criticism aimed against them. This means that the thesis of the exclusivity of communal obligations as a basis for one's duty to one's community must be rejected. It would seem that communal obligations supply an additional, but not the only, foundation for this duty.[91]

---

[91] The central reason why Dworkin wishes to understand political obligation as a communal one has to do with the support that such a conception provides for his jurisprudence, in his view. According to Dworkin's jurisprudence, a law not-only means the explicit decisions made in the past by the society's political institutions, but also all of the standards following from the principles guiding those past decisions (*ibid.*, p. 188). Dworkin believes that such a conception of law is appropriate to a society possessed of communal fraternity, and only such a society can meet the conditions required for the arisal of communal obligations, including the duty to obey the law. As the only way of supporting the legitimacy of government and the duty to obey it is through communal obligation, it follows that only

Moreover, if the duty to obey the law forms the central core of one's duty to his or her community, then it is not only the case that communal obligations are not the only possible basis for the duty to obey. Indeed, *it is impossible* for them to be such a basis. This is so, as it is not at all clear why the boundaries of people's communal obligations should be identical with the borderlines of their countries. Some of the communities to which people belong are smaller than their countries, while others span international borders. Furthermore, this is so, as even if there are communal obligations that are in exact agreement with the borders of the political community, thus making them a possible basis for political obligation, it is not at all clear how to justify the move from these obligations to the duty to obey the law. It would seem that the only bridges allowing for such a move are to be found in the argument from the negative consequences of disobedience, the argument from fairness, and the argument based on the duty to support just institutions. I intimated as much in discussing the last argument, and I shall now clarify my point.

Political obligation and the duty to obey the law are usually conceived of as synonyms. This book's first chapter includes a discussion of the differences between them. The concept of political obligation stresses precisely what the concept of the duty to obey fails to stress. It emphasizes the intimate link between the citizen and the political community to which he or she belongs, and the duty this citizen has to this community. On the other hand, the concept of political obligation, unlike that of the duty to obey, is a vague one in terms of the actions performance of which is required on its account. And yet, when political obligation is proven through justifications

the conception of the law offered by Dworkin is consistent with and supports the legitimacy of the law and the duty to obey it. His thesis that the duty to obey the law can be justified only as a communal duty, and in no other way, thus forms a premise of the argument for his central thesis on the nature of law as standards following from the principles underlying the positive rules created by political institutions. It is subordinated to this argument, then. As I am attempting to show within the chapter, even if communal obligations can indeed serve as grounds or as part of the grounds for the duty to obey the law and the legitimacy of government, they are not, and cannot be, the only possible basis for this duty. This is one reason for doubting the solidity of the support received by Dworkin's view of law, from his attempt to derive the duty to obey from communal obligations. Another reason casting doubt on its solidity is the fact that communal obligations may also arise in societies whose conception of law is not Dworkinean. In a society where a consensus of values exists between the members, and where the legal system is viewed as a system of rules dealing with the enforcement of these values and with the settlement of those areas of practical life on which these values are indifferent, there may be fraternity that gives rise to duties of communal association, including the duty to protect the law as a tool for enforcing the accepted values.

other than those demonstrating the duty to obey the law directly, when it is proven through justifications that substantiate one's duty of loyalty to the community, then the contender must also list the considerations allowing for identification of the actions required by this duty. To recapitulate: a contender who demonstrates the existence of a duty to obey the law, in an attempt to substantiate political obligation, is required to show that the duty to obey so proven is a citizen's duty, owed uniquely to his or her community. By the same token, a contender for the existence of political obligation on the basis of a duty of intimacy between citizen and community must prove that the contents of this duty include, among other things, the duty to obey the law.

Dworkin doesn't fulfill this requirement. He takes the matter for granted. But there are no grounds for doing so. When the matter under discussion is obligations to family and friends, the actions which these are obligations to perform are defined, first and foremost, by the needs and wishes of the men and women participating in these ties.[92] A similar strategy should be employed, perhaps, in the context of communal obligations. The needs and wishes of the community members should be consulted, in order to learn the contents of the citizen's obligations to this community. The duty to obey the law may well be included among these needs and wishes, but this must be demonstrated. Dworkin provides no such demonstration.

The link between political obligation, as based on communal obligations, and the duty to obey the law, may only, I think, be completed through use of a scaffolding comprising the argument from consequences, the argument from fairness and the duty to support just institutions. A community needs a legal system, and disobedience damages such a system for the reasons listed above in the discussion of these arguments. In order to show that political obligation which he has based on communal obligations is translatable into a duty to obey the law, Dworkin must accordingly give up his claim that communal obligations are the only possible basis for the duty to obey the law.

Communal obligations only substantiate the duty to obey the law in combination with the other arguments substantiating this duty. As I already showed towards the end of the previous section, these arguments supply an adequate explanation for the extent to which

---

[92] These needs and desires will at least form the raw data processed through the interpretative attitude of the people involved in the fraternal relationship, affording concrete duties within its framework.

the duty to obey is a unique duty owed by citizens to their communities. However, there is no doubt that communal obligations supply an even firmer basis for this relationship. It turns out that a single complex combining all four arguments supplies the firmest and most successful basis for political obligation. The argument from consequences, the argument from fairness and the argument based on the duty to support just institutions, clarify just why obeying the law is the central component of this obligation's substance. The argument from fairness and, to a larger extent, the argument from communal obligations, clarify just why this duty is mainly a unique and intimate duty owed by citizens to the specific communities of which they are members. The argument from consequences and the argument from the duty to support just institutions demonstrate why it is not only such a duty.

7. ON THE IMPORTANCE OF THE DUTY TO OBEY THE LAW

I have tried to show, in this chapter, that despite the criticism of many contemporary writers, some of the arguments offered by philosophical tradition as foundations for the duty to obey the law, indeed succeed in doing so. They succeed in supplying foundations for a duty which is mainly, though not only one owed by a citizen to the community of which he or she is a member. They succeed in supplying foundations for a universal duty as regards its subjects; a duty which applies to *everyone*. They do not, however, succeed in supplying foundations for it as a universal duty in the sense that the reasons supporting it are always present.[93]

---

[93] Perhaps this point should be re-distinguished from the one clarified in the first chapter, above, that is, from the point that even when the duty to obey applies, its absoluteness is limited, and it may be overridden by other considerations. To sum up, then, in saying that there is a duty to obey the law, we aren't saying that we are necessarily bound to perform every particular action required by the law. This is due to two conceptual considerations between which it is important to distinguish. First, when a certain type of action is considered a duty, this doesn't mean that it is required by reasons of absolute power relative to any possible reasons for action. It is required by reasons which are of absolute power only relative to specific, other reasons for action. Thus, reasons for action which do not fall under the absolute dominance of the reasons justifying the duty to obey the law may compete with this duty and override it. The weight it brings to bear against them will be discussed in the fourth chapter below. Second, as explained here, the fact that a specific type of action is viewed as a duty doesn't entail that all of the particular actions included in this type are required by reasons due to which this type is a duty. Accordingly, it may be the case that an action required by the law will not be performed, not only because the reasons justifying the duty to obey the law are overridden with regard to that action by other reasons, but also because the reasons justifying the duty to obey the law do not require this particular action at all.

Some of the authors mentioned here have tried, mainly on the basis of this lack of universality, to deny the existence of a duty to obey and support a position of philosophical anarchism, which would seem to have proved rather toothless.[94] If its propounders wished to bear new tidings, and the term "anarchism" creates expectations for fairly dramatic tidings, I think they should have shown that the duty to obey cannot be used in cases where it plays a significant role in the moral and political discourse, and in which it has an important practical meaning. Instead, the critical anarchists focused on trivial and esoteric contexts, jaywalking at three o'clock in the morning, in which the duty to obey is rarely cited anyway in the moral and political discourse, and to which no one seems to attach much importance. Moreover, these authors, of whom Raz and Simmons are central examples, did so only to return to acceptance of the important practical implications of the duty to obey, in cases which are the main ones requiring recourse to this duty in the political discourse.[95] These are usually cases in which laws are conceived of as bad or faulty, but in which disobedience has negative consequences for the institution of law in general, cases where disobedience means unfairness in the distribution of the burdens involved in maintaining this institution, and expresses a lack of solidarity with the political community.

I have claimed that these aspects of disobedience, along with a reliable conception of the concept of a generic duty, may serve as concrete foundations for continued adherence to the view that there is a duty to obey the law. However, from the point of view of their practical implications, my conclusions hardly differ from those of the anarchists. As stated, their denial of the duty to obey the law doesn't entail a moral permit to ignore, altogether, the fact that actions are required by law.[96] Conversely, the corroboration that I have tried to provide for the existence of this duty doesn't entail the conclusion that the fact that an action is required by law is one that always invokes a moral reason due to which this action is obligatory. Nonetheless, though, if there is a choice on the matter, it would seem preferable to interpret people's views on practical issues in the way which best supports their practical implications, rather than rejecting

---

[94] The identification of their stance as anarchism is anchored in some of their own expressions. See Raz, "Authority and Consent," and also Simmons, *Moral Principles and Political Obligations*, p. 195.

[95] Raz, *The Authority of Law*, p. 262; Simmons, *Moral Principles and Political Obligations*, p. 193.

[96] *Ibid.*

these views and then resurrecting all their significant practical ramifications, in the manner of the anarchists. I hope I have succeeded in showing the duty to obey the law to belong to this category.

I'll now add a few remarks on the importance of the duty to obey the law. M. B. E. Smith, one of the disbelievers in its existence, contends that even if it did exist, it would not be important. He concludes this from two criteria which he suggests for the evaluation of duties' importance. "First, that a *prima facie* obligation is a serious one if, and only if, an act which violates that obligation and fulfills no other is seriously wrong; and, second, that a *prima facie* obligation is a serious one if, and only if, violation of it will make considerably worse an act which on other grounds is already wrong."[97]

Smith cites the above-mentioned example of the law that prohibits crossing a street at 2 a.m. when the stoplight is red as evidence that the duty to obey is unimportant, according to his standards. And yet, what this example actually demonstrates is only that some cases of the duty to obey the law are trivial and unimportant. It doesn't show that the whole range of this duty's application is unimportant. In any case, it would be a mistake to draw conclusions regarding the general value of the duty to obey the law from the triviality of specific applications of it. Some, and even many, legal duties are trivial as the risk under which they place the values protected by the duty to obey depends on empirical probabilities that change from one instance of disobedience to another. In this sense, legal duties are no different from promissory obligations. The value that lies in the existence of an institution for the determination and enforcement of conducts within society will be placed under different risks in different instances of disobedience, just as the value that lies in the preservation of a system of interpersonal reliances will be placed under different risks in different instances of breach of promise. It does not follow from this that the general duties to obey the law and keep promises are unimportant. It is easy to point out examples of specific legal duties that are highly important according to Smith's own standards. (For instance, the duty to serve in the army when required to, for periods of time that are not needed for purposes of national security.)

Moreover, Smith's criteria are incomplete. First, it is true that his second criterion shows the duty to obey to be relatively less important

---

[97] See Smith, "Is There a *Prima Facie* Obligation to Obey the Law?," p. 970.

than the duty to keep promises and the duty to refrain from homicide. And yet, vis-à-vis this criterion, we must remind ourselves of another criterion of importance already intimated above; a moral duty is important if it is capable of rendering necessary and positive actions which would be negative, in the absence of this duty. It seems that the duty to obey the law gets higher grades on this than either of the other duties. Second, general duties (as opposed to the particular instances falling under them) are important if they protect important values, and the duty to obey the law (just like the duty to keep promises) indeed does so. Third and last, the importance of general duties is a function not only of the general values which they protect, but also of the frequency with which they will or may apply, and the frequency with which our actual lives encounter the reasons dominated by these duties. Our minor wishes are trivial and unimportant by virtue of their definition as minor. But our minor wishes are frequently present in the course of our daily lives. If a given general duty dominates them, then when the instances of this duty's application are very frequent, the fact that we are bound by this duty is an important fact of our lives, even if this duty doesn't protect important values. This is so, as being bound by such a duty means that when it applies, we do not permit ourselves to act on reasons that very frequently determine our actions.

The duty to obey the law (just like the duty to keep promises) is important by all these standards. The instances in which it has occasion to apply occur frequently; the reasons which it necessarily overrides, even if we are minimalists of the type who see these as merely minor wishes, also arise very frequently in our daily lives; finally, as I have already tried to maintain, this duty protects an important value: the existence of a mechanism for the institution and enforcement of desirable conducts, a mechanism whose existence enhances the stability and security of our lives, substantially.

This then is the importance of the duty to obey the law. Now to the limitations of this importance. It should be kept in mind that although the value protected by this duty is an important one, it isn't the most important one. Moreover, it is a value the importance of which is necessarily secondary to and parasitic upon other values. The foundations of the duty to obey discussed above base it on a conception of the law as a social tool. The value of any tool necessarily depends on the value of the goals for which it is used, and on the efficiency of this tool in attaining these goals. The law, as stated, is a tool for the institution and enforcement of desirable conducts. Its value, and the duty to obey it, thus necessarily depend on the fact of its efficient institution and enforcement of the desirable conducts.

All of the arguments discussed here and offering various bases for the duty to obey are dominated by this point. The argument from consequences is dominated by it, as the negative consequences to which it refers are, as clarified in detail above, the negative consequences that disobedience to the law may cause the functioning of the institution of *law as a tool for the institution and enforcement of desirable conducts*. The argument from fairness is dominated by it, as this argument has to do with the fair distribution of the burden that society members must bear in order to maintain the institution of *law as a tool for the institution and enforcement of desirable conducts*. The argument from the duty to support just institutions is dominated by it, as it has to do with supporting *just institutions*. It thus doesn't apply as a basis for the duty to obey unjust institutions. The argument from communal obligations is dominated by the present point, as this is an argument for political obligation, and it can only serve as a basis for the duty to obey in combination with one or more of the other arguments mentioned above.

The fact that all the grounds for the duty to obey discussed in this chapter are subordinated to the substantive values and goals furthered in practice by the institution of law, is one that is presupposed by the answers which I shall give to two central questions to be discussed in the following chapters. First, when a political system as a whole furthers unworthy values, how does this affect the general duty to obey the laws of this system? This is a question that will be discussed in the third chapter, below. Second, what are the standards on whose basis one should consider the fact that a given law furthers unworthy values, as reason for breaking this law and, consequently, going against the duty to obey in this context? This is a question that will be discussed in the last chapter of this book.

CHAPTER 3

The conditions of the applicability of the duty to obey the law and its democratic foundation

When a political system serves unworthy values, how does this fact affect the duty to obey its laws? The latest debate on this subject, between theoreticians of law and state, dealt with a subgroup of such political systems, i.e. with unjust and undemocratic systems. Furthermore, it was conducted on a background of humanist and liberal value systems. However, the logic of the arguments presented in this debate applies to more than just political systems which are tainted by injustice. It also applies to systems which are tainted by other important types of moral faults. Moreover, this logic is suited not only to humanism and liberalism. It is also suited to other types of value systems.

I point this out at the beginning of my present discussion, as this chapter will, for the most part, revolve on this debate, and will thus generally be conducted in terms of justice and democracy. It is important to note, and I shall return to this point, that this debate, in abstraction, may be applied to any important moral value, not only to those of justice and democracy, and to any value system, not only those of humanism and liberalism.

In the debate I'm referring to, that between Simmons and Rawls, the latter is of the opinion that gross injustice on the part of the political system renders the duty to obey its laws void *ab initio*.[1] The former, on the other hand, sees such injustice as a permanent source of reasons for disobedience. These reasons may override the duty to obey in many cases, but they do not cancel its basic validity *ab initio*.[2] These two views will be discussed in the first part of this chapter.

A non-democratic political system necessarily suffers from a serious

---

[1] Rawls, *A Theory of Justice*, p. 112. This position may also be ascribed to Locke (*Second Treatise on Civil Government*, sections 131 and 135). See also David Richards, *A Theory of Reasons For Action* (Oxford: Oxford University Press, 1971), pp. 152–3.

[2] See Simmons, *Moral Principles and Political Obligations*, p. 78.

fault as regards its justness.[3] The fact that a political system is of this type should accordingly affect the duty to obey its laws in the same manner that any other grave injustice should affect this duty. The presence of democracy in a political system will prevent these effects. However, the presence of democracy has another effect, besides prevention of the results of its absence. I mentioned this point at the beginning of the last chapter: the fact that a political system is a democracy provides additional and special reasons for obeying its laws. These reasons will be discussed in the second part of this chapter.

Insufficient attention has been paid, in philosophical literature, to the distinction between the two ways in which democracy affects the duty to obey the law. I'm referring to the distinction between the fact that *democracy's absence from the political system disqualifies the duty to obey its laws* or provides reasons for disobeying them, and the fact that *its presence adds new reasons for obedience*, besides preventing the presence of reasons for disobedience or disqualification of the duty to obey. On the one hand, those who argue the case of the special reasons which democracy provides for obeying the law consider the general reasons for obedience (such as consent, the argument from consequences and fairness) applicable to unjust and undemocratic forms of government as well.[4] On the other hand, those who address the question whether or not the general reasons for obedience apply to unjust and undemocratic systems as well offer no separate arguments for the existence of any special reasons for obedience, stemming from democracy.[5] Neglect of the present distinction obscures the emphasis often placed by philosophers and non-philosophers on the importance of obeying the law within democracies.[6] It is thus especially important to stress this distinction. This is the main reason why I am combining

---

[3] This, at least, is the position prevalent among both theorists and laymen. It is based on reasons connected with equality, liberty and autonomy. I am not attempting here to discuss the grounding provided by these reasons for the stance that a lack of democracy amounts to a serious flaw in the justness of a political system, or the separate question whether this is so only *prima facie*. Such a discussion far exceeds the boundaries of this chapter's present section, which deals with the arguments relating to the effects of a system's unjustness upon the duty to obey it.

[4] See Peter Singer, *Democracy and Disobedience* (Oxford: Oxford University Press, 1973), pp. 17–20; John Plamenatz, *Consent, Freedom and Political Obligation*, 2nd edition (Oxford: Oxford University Press, 1968), Introduction, p. vii.

[5] E.g. Rawls, *A Theory of Justice*; Simmons, *Moral Principles and Political Obligations*.

[6] For instance, the Australian Prime Minister is quoted by Singer as saying, "As to inciting people to break the law, I think there can be no excuse whatsoever for this in a community where the opportunity exists to change the law through the ballot box." See Singer,

a discussion of justice and democracy as conditions for obedience, on the one hand, with one of democracy as an independent source of reasons for obedience, on the other.

I. JUSTICE AND DEMOCRACY AS CONDITIONS FOR THE DUTY TO OBEY THE LAW

Surprising though it may be, the controversy as to whether justice and democracy are conditions for the duty to obey the law is quite a new one. In fact, it can hardly even be called a controversy as yet. Till very recently, at least as regards the injustice consisting of the absence of democracy, what the literature yielded was either statements of the position that the general arguments for the duty to obey discussed in the previous chapters apply not only in democracies,[7] or statements to the contrary.[8] These were barely supported by argumentation of any kind and there was certainly no exchange of critical comments between the two positions, meriting the title of controversy. All of this holds for the period prior to John Simmons' attack against Rawls' claim that the principle of fairness, which requires obedience to the law, cannot apply to unjust and undemocratic political systems.[9]

Rawls expresses the view that "it is not possible to have an obligation to autocratic and arbitrary forms of government" as part and an entailment of the more general idea, that "by the principle of fairness it is not possible to be bound to unjust institutions."[10] This claim is not restricted to the duty to obey the law based solely upon

---

Democracy and Disobedience, p. 1. This type of statement is very familiar, and I won't bother here to quote similar comments made by Israeli leaders. T. H. Green says,

> Supposing then the individual to have decided that some command of a "political superior" is not for the common good, how ought he to act in regard to it? In a country like ours, with a popular government and settled methods of enacting and repealing laws, the answer of common sense is simple and sufficient. He should do all he can by legal methods to get the command canceled, but till it is canceled, he should conform to it. (Green, *Lectures on the Principles of Political Obligation* [London: Longmans, 1907], section 100, p. 111.)

It is unclear whether the emphasis placed by these two quotations on the duty to obey the law in democracies indicates that such a duty exists only in democracies, or whether this duty is only more binding there. It is also unclear whether what makes this duty more binding is the added support afforded it by additional reasons, or the absence of reasons against it which are present in undemocratic regimes.

[7] E.g. Singer, *Democracy and Disobedience*, pp. 17–20; Plamenatz, *Consent, Freedom and Political Obligation*, Introduction, p. vii.   [8] E.g. Rawls, *A Theory of Justice*, p. 112.

[9] See also Greenawalt, *Conflicts of Law and Morality*, pp. 129–33.

[10] Rawls, *A Theory of Justice*, p. 112.

the principle of fairness. It also applies when this duty is grounded upon its other justifications (e.g. the argument from consequences). Furthermore, as stated above, it is not only part of and implied by the idea that one cannot be under obligation to unjust institutions. It is also part of and follows from the more general idea that it is impossible to have an obligation to immoral and not merely unjust institutions. These two extensions, that is, of the effect of the justice condition (on the validity of the duty to obey in the context of *all its grounds* and not only that of its fairness foundations), and of the breadth of its basis (in other words, the fact of its stemming not only from injustice but also from immorality), follow, as we shall see shortly, from the argument forming the basis of the thesis that justice forms a condition for the validity of the duty to obey.

This argument is based on an analogy to "the generally agreed view that extorted promises are void *ab initio*." According to Rawls, "unjust social arrangements are themselves a kind of extortion, even violence, and consent to them does not bind."[11] Though the argument is brief and undetailed, it is perfectly complete. Simmons begins his criticism of it with an attack on the analogy between unjust institutions and extorted promises. The latter are void *ab initio*. But they are void as they were not undertaken voluntarily, while "the injustice of an institution need not affect the voluntariness of one's consent to it. Supposing only that the unjust institution does not happen to be doing violence to me, I can freely consent to its authority."[12]

Though this line of criticism seems perfectly correct, it has no bearing at all upon the thesis concerning the justice condition. Instead of drawing an analogy from extorted promises to unjust institutions, we should simply draw one from promises to commit immoral acts. Such promises, though they are made voluntarily, are void *ab initio*.[13] Thus, the fact that one may consent voluntarily to

---

[11] *Ibid.*, p. 343.   [12] Simmons, *Moral Principles and Political Obligations*, p. 78.

[13] As Simmons himself notes, "a promise to aid [a person] in his villainy, of course, would not bind us" (*ibid.*). One may say that the capacity of promises' involuntariness to bring about their cancellation, and the capacity of their immorality to do so, act on separate levels. The involuntariness of an utterance or a gesture of promise undermine the very success of the utterance or the gesture in becoming promises, while the immorality of a promise annuls its binding nature. In other words, promises obtained through extortion aren't promises at all, while immoral promises are promises, but non-binding ones. Those who view the connection between promises and duties as an analytic one will have difficulty in making this distinction. They will claim that both involuntary and immoral promises are actually not promises. However, in the present context, and in fact for all practical purposes, the present

unjust institutions does not imply that such consent gives rise to obligations, as *it is the institution's unjustness, rather than the involuntary nature of consent to it* that renders such obligations void *ab initio*.

Simmons, who is aware of this possible strategy for defending the justice condition, offers three arguments against it. The first is based on an analogy between consent to unjust institutions and promises made to villains. The second relies on the claim that "the intuitive force of the principle of fair play seems to be preserved even for, e.g., criminal conspiracies."[14] The third is grounded on the idea that fairness requires us to return in proportion to goods in fact received, without worrying about the moral qualities of those who provide them.

The first argument seems to me "to be a good illustration of the dangers of metaphor."[15] Simmons believes that adopting a position according to which we cannot be under obligation to unjust institutions, will "commit [us...] to the position that a promise to an unscrupulous villain does not bind,"[16] a position which, as Simmons rightly judges, is totally absurd. However, are we really committed to such a position by the view that there cannot be a duty to obey unjust institutions? I believe not.

There are significant differences between the duty to obey an unjust institution and the duty to keep a promise made to a villain. They totally undermine the analogy between the two. Moreover, they strengthen the thesis that the application of the duty to obey should be restricted to just institutions only. These differences lie, firstly, in the ways in which particular acts fall under each of these two general duties, and, secondly, in the foundations of our relationships with the subjects to whom these two duties are owed.

As regards the first point, an act which we promise to perform is an act which we are bound to perform *because we have promised it.* Consequently, *we are in full command of the nature of this act.* Being the promisors, it is we who determine its contents. In failing to exclude villains from the scope of the general duty to keep promises, we are not granting them moral power which they may utilize to commit injustices. The duty to obey institutions is utterly different. It is a duty to perform acts *because the institution to which this duty is owed*

distinction seems to make very little difference. For if the binding obligation of a promise is canceled, of what importance is it whether this follows from the fact that the promise was no promise in the first place or from the fact that it was merely non-binding?

[14] Simmons, *Moral Principles and Political Obligations*, p. 110.   [15] *Ibid.*, p. 78.
[16] *Ibid.*, p. 78.

demands their performance.[17] In acknowledging such a duty to a given institution, we grant it the moral power to assign us particular duties, without retaining any control of their creation or contents. Thus, in failing to exclude unjust institutions from the scope of the general duty to obey the law, we will be granting unjust institutions moral power which they may abuse directly. Such a move seems far more drastic than acknowledging the duty to keep promises to villains.

It may be argued that acknowledging a generic duty to obey an institution doesn't mean granting this institution the power to create absolute reasons for actions, but only reasons of limited absoluteness.[18] Accordingly, acknowledging such a generic duty doesn't mean a loss of control over the answer to the question whether or not to perform these actions. This fact may serve to rescue the attempt to argue for the thesis that there is a duty to obey unjust institutions. However, and despite this fact, there is still a marked difference between acknowledging such a duty and acknowledging a generic duty to keep promises to villains. In acknowledging the latter, we are not granting the villains the power to create the promises and determine their contents. In acknowledging the duty to obey unjust institutions, we are doing just this. And although this doesn't mean we have granted them the power to dictate our actions, we have granted them the power to affect the balance of reasons according to which we determine our actions. Thus the question remains, why grant unjust institutions such powers?

Further, and this is the second point of difference between acknowledging a duty to obey an institution and a duty to keep promises to villains: unlike natural humans, who are, of themselves, of value, institutions are not, it would seem, possessed of such intrinsic value. Institutions seem to draw their value from the purposes served by them, from the degree of efficiency with which they serve these purposes, and from the degree of their justice. Institutions serving immoral or unjust purposes cannot but have negative value from the moral point of view, as they have no other source from which they may draw moral value. The duty to obey institutions is based on the instrumentality of obedience to the preservation of these institutions, and on the requirement for equal distribution of the burdens involved in such preservation. And yet, why should morality require us to

---

[17] On this matter, see chapter 1, above, pp. 14–18, and also chapter 2, pp. 75–8.
[18] On this see chapter 1, above, pp. 20–1.

contribute equally to the preservation of institutions whose existence is of no moral value, or worse yet, of institutions whose existence is of a morally negative value?

The situation is entirely different as regards promises made to humans. Humans are possessed of intrinsic moral value which exceeds their goals and characters. Excluding classes of humans, due to their goals or character, from the scope to which specific moral obligations apply, amounts to a denial of their intrinsic value. We exclude from the scope of morality obligations whose observance will supply direct assistance to villainous activities. (Promises to assist villains in their villainous acts are not morally binding, as Simmons concedes.) The duty to obey unjust institutions seems to bear a closer relation to this type of duties than it does to keeping promises to villains. The latter are not necessarily unjust. The former are. So too is the duty to obey unjust institutions. If we conceive of promises to perform unjust acts as void *ab initio*, then, we must conceive of the duty to obey unjust institutions in precisely the same way.

Further significant differences can be pointed out between obeying unjust institutions and keeping promises to villains.[19] However, I shall not do so here, as the above-mentioned differences seem sufficiently solid to support an analogy between unjust promises and unjust institutions. If there can be no obligation to keep the former, then neither can there be any obligation to obey the latter.[20] This applies to political obligation not because of what distinguishes injustice from other types of immorality, but rather, because injustice is a sort of immorality. And despite the impression created by Rawls' formulations and the context in which his claims are presented, this applies to the duty to obey the law not only when it is based on

---

[19] For example, if we exclude villains from the group of people to whom the duty to keep promises applies, and the villains know that we don't keep the promises we make them, then we lose an important channel through which we may influence villains to change their ways. There is no argument analogous to this one against excluding unjust institutions from the group of institutions to which the duty to obey the law applies.

[20] Greenawalt doubts the voidness of immoral promises (*Conflicts of Law and Morality*, pp. 84–5). He uses this claim in order to argue that one can be bound by fairness to unjust institutions (*ibid.*, p. 132). His argument that immoral promises are capable of binding relies on an example of a promise to tell a white lie in order to aid a friend. In Greenawalt's opinion, such a promise may be binding. The persuasive force of this example, if it indeed possesses such force, is limited to promises whose immorality is not gross immorality, and which are given in the context of friendship, so that the duty to keep them is not merely a duty to keep promises, but also a duty of friendship. Subsequently, the persuasive force of this example as regards the annulment of the duty to obey in the context of systems suffering from gross immorality is extremely doubtful.

fairness, but when it is based on the argument from negative consequences as well.

It is of interest that while Rawls seems to believe that it is the duty to obey based on considerations of fairness especially which is subject to the justice condition, Simmons' second and third objections are intended to show just the opposite. They set out to show that especially in the context of the argument from fairness, the duty to obey is exempt from the justice condition. Furthermore, his first criticism of the restriction of the duty to obey the law to just communities only was based on an attempt to show that this duty, like the one to keep promises to villains and unlike the one to keep villainous promises, is not necessarily immoral and is thus not void *ab initio*. His second criticism is intended to demonstrate that even if this duty were necessarily a duty to perform immoral acts, it would not be rendered invalid by this.

This criticism is based on what Simmons views as our basic intuitions about the fairness principle.[21] He believes that by these intuitions, the fairness principle even applies in criminal gangs.[22] This thesis is true in a sense, but not in the moral sense. When a member of a gang refuses to share the profits of a robbery with his colleagues, his villainy is twofold. And yet it is not at all clear whether the latter can enlist the aid of morality against him. It is obvious that morality cannot be expected to support the existence of criminal gangs. Consequently, it will either be silent on the issue of mutually unfair behavior between the members of such a gang, or it will actually strive to encourage such unfairness and mistrust in the interests of actively undermining the gang's stability.

When the justice condition is referred to as restricting the scope of the duty to obey the law, two additional important points must be noted. First, this condition is not intended to discourage the "backward looking" fairness of unjust institutions, having to do with the equal distribution of the profits of crimes committed. It is intended, rather, to discourage the "forward looking" fairness pertaining to the undertaking of burdens necessary for the amassment of profits from further crimes. Subsequently, though the characters we view with the most distaste in Westerns are invariably those who are even villainous towards their colleagues, those who free ride the benefits of robbery and murder, it is nonetheless clear that the way to

---

[21] Greenawalt is party to the general tone of this criticism. *Ibid.*, p. 132.
[22] Simmons, *Moral Principles and Political Obligations*, p. 110.

absolve oneself of former sins is not continued participation in subsequent crimes. Second, the justice condition is intended to encourage disobedience to unjust institutions that stems from moral, rather than egotistic reasons. Villains who cease to carry out the tasks of their gang as they wish to give up their criminal careers, and not because they wish to profit at the expense of their colleagues, can hardly be considered free riders. They do not break the rules of fair play even in the limited sense in which they are broken by members of a gang who evade the tasks of robbery and then attempt to share in the profits gained through these tasks. The breach committed by the former expresses no wish to play unfairly. What it expresses is a wish to stop playing altogether, and this is what the justice condition sets out to achieve. Not unfair play at immoral games but, rather, complete abstinence from such games.

In his third criticism of the move to restrict the validity of the duty to obey the law to just institutions,[23] Simmons switches from the conception of the fairness argument as one of distributive justice, the conception implicit in his former criticism, to a conception of it as an argument of corrective justice.[24] According to Simmons' former claims, distributive justice is required even of immoral societies, while the present criticism implies that corrective justice is required despite the immorality of societies lacking distributive justice. The motive behind the justice condition is, Simmons contends, the idea that "it is unfair to demand full cooperation from one to whom full benefits are denied."[25] In other words, one doesn't have to pay for more than one receives. If this is truly the idea behind the justice condition, then Simmons is correct in claiming that this does not entail the voidness *ab initio* of the duty to obey unjust institutions. What follows from this idea is that within such institutions "those who are allocated the largest shares of benefits owe the largest share of burdens" and that "even one who is allocated a very small share of the benefits is bound to carry a small share of the burdens."[26] Simmons, however, is wrong in construing the motivating force behind the justice condition in terms of the corrective justice conception of the principle of fairness. As I explained in the previous chapter, the idea underlying the principle of fairness when it serves as grounds for the duty to obey is not that one should give return for goods received, but rather that one should do so as part of a just arrangement, an arrangement by

[23] See also Greenawalt, *Conflicts of Law and Morality*, p. 132.
[24] On these two conceptions of the argument from fairness, see chapter 2, notes 44–45.
[25] Simmons, *Moral Principles and Political Obligations*, p. 112.   [26] *Ibid.*, p. 113.

which the burdens and benefits involved in the goods' production are distributed equally.[27] Rather than rejecting the justice condition for not following from the corrective justice conception of the fairness principle, it is this conception of the principle that should be rejected for not allowing room for the justice condition. For what is relevant to this condition and to the principle of fairness in our context, is not just the fairness of a particular individual to whoever awards him or her benefits, but this fairness as part of the justice of society as a whole. Accordingly, even those who receive a large portion of the goods produced by an unjust system are not obliged to obey such a system. What should follow from the justice condition is not only that the blacks of South Africa are not obliged by fairness to South African law, but also that the whites are not.

When the thesis of the voidness *ab initio* of the duty to obey for unjust and undemocratic governments is supported by the similarity between such governments and immoral promises, it would seem to prove solid enough to withstand Simmons' attacks. This does not mean, though, that this thesis is not in need of some amount of qualification. I shall contend that the effect of the immorality of the political system upon the duty to obey its laws may be overriden by other considerations. Before clarifying and substantiating this claim, I would like to point out a certain feature of the controversy between the positions represented by Simmons and Rawls, a feature which I consider quite significant. This controversy involves two issues, rather than one. It not only entails different answers to the question whether or not the absence of democracy or other serious moral faults in political institutions can be overriden by other considerations. It also entails different answers to the question, at what stage must the first question be answered. While Rawls' position indicates that this question must be answered upon deciding whether or not there is a general duty to obey the laws of a given political system, Simmons' view indicates that this question must be answered upon deciding whether or not to obey a specific law in a given undemocratic system. This last conclusion, implied by Simmons' position, must be rejected outright. It would seem to involve a confusion as to the very concept of the duty to obey the law.

This duty means a duty to perform acts commanded by laws because they are so commanded, or in other words *because norms belonging to the legal system require their performance*.[28] Were this not the

---

[27] See chapter 2, note 45.   [28] On this matter see chapter 1, above, pp. 14–18.

case, the duties to perform these acts would be independent of the fact of being required by laws. They would not be duties to obey the law. The question whether there is a duty to obey the law is a question about the political system, then about the institution of law, and only via this is it also a question about the individual laws composing the law as an institution and a system. The duty to obey may only be justified in terms of the arguments discussed in the previous chapter, all of which focus upon law as an institution.[29] This means that the duty to obey the laws of a specific legal system presupposes the moral desirability of this institution. As the moral features of a legal system, the values and goals which it serves, are what determine its moral desirability, these features first affect the answer to the question whether there is a general duty to obey this system, and only through this do they answer the question whether to perform the acts required by its individual laws.

To reinforce the last point, we may remind ourselves that the duty to obey the law is of real practical significance chiefly in cases where acts are required by bad laws. Acts required by good laws, be they acts whose omission is *mala per se*, or acts which contribute to the production of public goods, are less in need of the support of the duty to obey the law.[30] In view of this, and if, as Simmons suggests, a system's injustice should be active at the point of deciding whether or not to obey its particular laws, what, should these be bad laws, might shift the balance against the lack of justice or the system's other negative features? What could, in such a case, redeem the acts required by these particular laws from the forces emanating from the system's immoral nature and opposing their performance? Could the faults of an individual law outweigh the unjustness of the entire system and serve as reason for performing the undesirable act required by this law? This is clearly nonsense.

What is it that might mislead one to the view that the immorality of a legal system should be weighed only at the stage when obedience to its individual laws is considered, and not at the stage when the existence of a general duty to obey the system is decided? Perhaps what causes this is the thought that a denial of the general duty to

---

[29] On this matter see chapter 2, above, p. 93.

[30] The examples through which Greenawalt attempts to demonstrate that the principle of fair play applies to unjust systems as well are just such examples – of particular laws contributing towards the creation of a public good. See Greenawalt, *Conflicts of Law and Morality*, pp. 129–30. He, thus, misses the distinction between the need to preserve the system as a whole, a need which might be invalid were the system unjust, and the need to preserve subsystems of it, a need which might be valid were these subsystems just.

obey a specific legal system due to its negative moral character would entail the voidness *ab initio* of all of the duties to perform the acts required by the system's individual laws. The analogy Simmons draws between the duty to obey unjust institutions and the duty to keep promises to villains corroborates this suspicion. What seems enticing about the analogy is the fact that just as promises to villains are not necessarily villainous, and just as the villainy of the promisee accordingly shouldn't entail the voidness *ab initio* of promises made him or her, the particular laws of unjust governments are not necessarily unjust and these governments' unjustness accordingly shouldn't entail the voidness *ab initio* of the duty to obey these laws.[31]

However, at this point in our discussion it should already be clear that such a line of thought is mistaken. This mistake is analogous to the previous one. For the same reason due to which the acknowledgment of the duty to obey the law is of practical significance chiefly in the context of acts required by faulty laws, the failure to acknowledge this duty is of little practical significance in the context of acts required by good laws. These laws, by definition, are laws that require actions whose omission is bad either because it harms others directly or because it may frustrate or damage the production of a public good. Considerations of consequences and considerations of fairness (either separately or jointly) give rise to duties to perform these actions whether or not they give rise to a duty to obey the political system generating the laws that require these actions. A denial of the latter duty doesn't imply a denial of the former ones. Consequently, a view of a system's lack of justice, or of its other morally negative features as causing the voidness *ab initio* of the duty to obey its laws, doesn't imply that there is no obligation whatsoever to perform the acts required by its good laws. Not acknowledging the duty to obey the laws of South Africa doesn't mean that we have no obligation whatsoever to perform acts required by this country's traffic regulations or its environmental laws.

Of course, the corruptness of political systems, besides giving reason not to support such systems and thus not to acknowledge the duty to obey their laws, can also give justification for an active struggle against these systems. Some may locate one of the ways of actualizing such a struggle in disobedience to the duties to perform the acts which their laws require. They will tell us, for instance, to drive on the left side of the road in Nazi Germany, to pollute its

---

[31] This also goes for Greenawalt's examples, *ibid.*, pp. 129–30.

rivers, and so forth, all in order to make living conditions there unbearable and thus bring about the collapse of the political system. For obvious reasons, this way of fighting corrupt political systems may be extremely impractical. This issue is, however, relatively unimportant in the present context. What is important here is the emphasis that the existence of a justification to fight immoral institutions and the absence of the duty to obey their laws are two, quite separate matters. They are logically and normatively unequivalent. While the former *might*, due to further considerations, be concretized by *breaking the good laws* of such systems, the second *must*, due to the very concept of the obligation to obey the law, express itself in ignoring and consequently *breaking their bad laws* and no more. Moreover, if the justification for fighting corrupt institutions also forms a justification to abstain from performing the acts required by these institutions' good laws, then it is likely that this justification will not be forced to compete with the duty to obey their laws. For if the degree of the political system's corruptness is such that it justifies a struggle against this system, even through disobeying duties to perform acts required by its good laws, then this degree of corruptness has obviously already justified the conclusion that the duty to obey the system's laws is void.

This matter restores us to the question with which we began; should the absence of democracy or other types of corruptness in political systems disqualify the duty to obey these systems outright? I hope that I have shown above that an affirmative answer to this question, based on an analogy to immoral promises, is the correct one. However, as I have already intimated, this answer is in need of some qualification. What it means is that gross injustice on the part of political systems must count as *prima facie*, but not absolute, reason for disqualifying the general duty to obey their laws. This is due to the fact that gross injustice on the part of political systems may form only part of the moral considerations to be taken into account in deciding the answer to the question whether or not they should be preserved. We may have an obligation to obey the law and support the government despite the fact that both suffer from grave moral defects, as the injustice caused by the government's and law's collapse may exceed that caused by their existence.[32] To see this, there is

---

[32] For a similar point see also Greenawalt, *ibid.*, p. 193. In the context of grounding the duty to obey on the principle of fairness, Greenawalt's view is, as we have seen, similar to

unfortunately no need to employ imagination. It was right, so I believe, to acknowledge the duty to obey Stalin while he was at war with Hitler. (Here it must, of course, be noted that acknowledging such a duty doesn't mean that one is obligated to run down Stalin's political opponents with one's car, under cover of darkness, even if so instructed. We must remind ourselves: acknowledging the duty to obey the laws of a given country doesn't mean acknowledging an absolute duty to do so. A non-absolute duty may also be outweighed by considerations pertaining to the substance of particular laws. There is both a theoretical and a practical difference between disobeying a specific law of Stalin's as we acknowledge no duty to obey it, and disobeying it as the duty to obey it is outweighed by the force of this particular law's criminality. The latter logically entails a willingness to perform, in Stalin's name, acts which are, of themselves, at least somewhat undesirable, for instance, the execution of an unwise economic policy, or of policies of doubtful strategic value. The former doesn't entail even this willingness.)

The following analogy may aid us in summarizing and clarifying much of what has been said so far. Picture a team of surgeons who share a single scalpel, and a gang of robbers who share a single switchblade. We clearly have a general obligation to preserve the scalpel and no such general obligation to preserve the switchblade. Suppose, though, that the robbers use the switchblade for other purposes besides robbery. Suppose they use it to combat a rival gang that specializes in murder. This fact may give rise to a general duty not to harm the switchblade. So far so good as to our general duties to the scalpel and the switchblade. These must be carefully distinguished, though, from the decisions which we should make about particular references to these instruments. Such decisions may be *affected* by the existence or non-existence of general duties, but they are not *dictated* by these duties. If a member of the surgery team tries to use the scalpel to slit open a personal letter addressed to one of his colleagues, this certainly isn't reason enough to damage the scalpel. The general duty to preserve the scalpel, a duty which we have acknowledged, overrides the value damaged by the scalpel's presently intended use, that is, the value of privacy. However, if one of the team members attempts murder with the scalpel, and the only means of

Simmons'. In other words, he believes that this duty applies to unjust and undemocratic systems as well. In the context of other grounds for the duty to obey, he approaches Rawls' position, with exceptions similar to those discussed in this chapter.

prevention is damaging the scalpel, then there is then undoubtedly very good reason to do so. This damage will not be caused because of the absence of a duty to preserve the scalpel. It will be caused because this duty is overridden under the present circumstances by the value to be damaged through the scalpel's specific imminent use. Now, back to the bandits. Though there may be no reason to preserve their knife, this doesn't mean that there is no reason to preserve those goods produced by it that are not immoral. If, besides being used for robbery, the switchblade was also used to prepare food, the fact that it need not be preserved doesn't mean that the food need not be preserved. This last point may be likened to the matter of the good laws produced by a corrupt legal system.

As stated above, the duty to obey, being an obligation to preserve an instrument and an obligation to undertake a fair share in this preservation, depends for its moral validity on the character of the political system towards which it is claimed to be binding. Thus, if a political system is either undemocratic or suffers from some other serious moral defect, and if these are not overridden by other considerations, then the general duty to obey the laws of this system is void *ab initio*. Note, it is the general duty to obey this system that is void, not only its *individual* applications. Conversely, if this *general* duty is not rendered void *ab initio*, this doesn't mean that it wins on all of its particular *applications*. Moreover, if the general duty to obey a given system is indeed void, this doesn't mean the subsequent voidness of any duty other than the duty to obey, to perform the acts required by this system's laws. Having an obligation to preserve a tool doesn't mean unconditional acceptance of all of its uses. Not having such an obligation doesn't mean the unconditional rejection of all of the tool's uses.

So much, then, for the negative effects of democracy's absence and of other forms of gross immorality on the duty to obey the law. I shall now turn to an examination of the positive effects of democracy's presence on this duty.

2. DEMOCRACY AS GROUNDS FOR THE DUTY TO OBEY

As stated at the beginning of this chapter, the fact that a political system is democratic is a fact that affects the duty to obey its laws beyond preventing the nullifying effects of democracy's absence, discussed above. Philosophers and others have claimed that democracy supplies additional and special reasons to obey the law, besides those that exist by virtue of the necessity of preserving the law as a tool for the enforcement and institution of desirable conducts. There are two main reasons of this type. One is related to democracy's very substance, the fact of its being a fair distribution of the community's normative powers of political influence. The other has to do with democracy as a procedure. People participate actively in democracy as a procedure. They at least vote. According to some, people place themselves, through this participation, under an obligation to accept the results of the elections.

Fair distribution of political power

The success of the argument that democracy supplies additional reasons for obedience, being a fair distribution of political power, naturally depends upon the soundness of the view that democracy, under which each adult has a single vote, is indeed such a fair distribution. This view is not free of problems. There have been and may yet be those who see a fair distribution of voting power as requiring that distinctions be made between citizens according to certain features or skills. John Stuart Mill's famous proposal that the educated be given two votes each is an expression of such a stance.[33] However, given the beliefs of most people, it seems that the problems endangering the present argument have to do with the transition from democracy's fairness to the conclusions regarding obedience, and not with issues of this type.

This is readily demonstrated by a look at Peter Singer's *Democracy and Disobedience*. This book includes a highly detailed analysis of our topic. Presenting democracy's fairness as the basis for the duty to obey, Singer focuses on the first issue mentioned above, that is, on the question whether democracy actually is a fair distribution of political power. He sets out to replace the commonly accepted conception of the fairness underlying the democratic principle, i.e. the conception of fairness as equality. The substitute he offers is a conception of this fairness as compromise. However, the central problems aroused by his discussion do not pertain to the question whether democracy is a fair distribution of political power, but rather to the question whether such fairness gives rise to special reasons for obeying the law. Whatever the correct manner of construing the fairness underlying democracy, Singer's explanation of the transition from this fairness to the conclusions concerning obedience is a muddled one.

[33] J. S. Mill, *Representative Government* (London: Dent, 1960), ch. 8.

It seems to oscillate between three alternative explanations. According to the first, as democracy is a fair compromise between rival demands, it must be obeyed so as *to be preserved*.[34] This explanation is sound enough, but it doesn't show how democracy gives rise to *additional* reasons for obeying the law. The reason that this explanation cites is based on the fact that the law is a tool for the institution and enforcement of desirable conducts, not on the fact that it is democratic. As I have shown in the first part of this chapter, *democracy may be considered a precondition for the applicability of this reason. It cannot be seen as its source.*[35]

According to another interpretation of Singer's position, as democracy is a fair compromise, it produces just laws and we are duty-bound to obey such laws.[36] This argument is obviously based on false assumptions. The fact that a decision is reached through a just procedure doesn't ensure the justness of this decision. This is already a commonplace of democratic theory.[37] Raz illustrates this point through an analogy: "[T]he fact that a decision was taken by an official who followed all the rules of natural justice does not render it just..."[38]

Raz, aware of the presence of these two explanations in Singer's discussion, rejects the thesis that democracy's fairness gives rise to special reasons for obedience. However, a third explanation is implicit in Singer's claims. According to this explanation, in disobeying the law in a democracy, one assumes "greater say than others have about what should be done."[39] In order to refrain from doing so, one must refrain from disobeying the law. Raz's analogy should, it seems, be inverted relative to this argument. The point, according to it, is not that a just procedure necessarily produces just decisions, but that the view that a given decision is desirable is not reason enough to depart

---

[34] Singer, *Democracy and Disobedience*, p. 36: "There are strong reasons for playing one's part in supporting and preserving a decision procedure which represents a fair compromise."

[35] According to Singer's own line of thought, democracy in the context of the present argument, need not be seen as a precondition for the present reason's application, but rather as a source of added weight to this general reason for obedience. For Singer himself believes that we have a duty to preserve the institution of the law, even if it isn't democratic.

[36] It was Raz who pointed out the possibility of this interpretation of Singer (Raz, *The Authority of Law*, p. 242). I am not completely convinced that this stance can actually be attributed to Singer. The closest formulation I have found is the following: "Fairness or justice are additional reasons for supporting a fair compromise when no fairer outcome can be reached" (Singer, *Democracy and Disobedience*, p. 37).

[37] See Rawls, *A Theory of Justice*, p. 356.   [38] Raz, *The Authority of Law*, p. 242.

[39] Singer, *Democracy and Disobedience*, p. 36.

from the just procedures which should be employed to reach this decision. Though the analogy is imperfect, it is roughly possible to say that just as the official's belief in the justness of a given solution to a dispute is not reason enough to take this decision while deviating from the rules of natural justice, so a person's belief in the desirability of a given solution to a practical problem occupying his or her community isn't reason enough for this person to act on this proposal while deviating from democratic procedures. Apart from being the means which, given the limitations of humanity, are often the best means available for arriving at correct decisions, democratic procedures, as well as the rules of natural justice, are of intrinsic value. They actualize principles of fairness and express respect towards human beings. They should consequently be adhered to. The force of democracy's inherent value, as that of the rules of natural justice, is at times sufficient to override the faults of decisions which might have been prevented had other procedures been employed.

It is important to be precise about the way in which the concept of law should be conceived of in the context of the present argument. "The law" cannot be conceived of here as an institution for determining desirable conducts, neither can it be conceived of as a particular norm. In fact, the last sense cannot underlie any claim that democracy provides special grounds for the duty to obey. Even if it were true, that the democratic procedure ensures just consequences, this could not constitute the reason to obey the law in democracies. First, not all the laws of democratic states are necessarily products of democratic procedures. Second, accepting this would raise the question as to what democratic procedure is relevant to the assessment of laws' justness. Is it the specific democratic procedure through which the laws under discussion were enacted, or perhaps the most recent democratic procedure, the last elections? If we are bound to obey the laws of democracies because the majority's support makes them just, then the present majority would seem to be what counts. But having to obey the present majority is something quite different from having to obey the law. Not every law in a democracy is necessarily a product of elections expressing the will of the present majority, and not every desire or belief held by the present majority is expressed by the law.[40]

---

[40] There may be some who will reply that the present majority has the power to change the laws with which it disagrees, and the power to give legal expression to its wishes, and that everything it wants is expressed by the law. However, this thesis is at least a little fictitious.

In the context of the argument from democracy, law, then, should be conceived of as representing the normative state of affairs of a community, as representing the store of decisive and authoritative solutions to its practical problems. When the law is conceived of in this manner, then it is clear that the power to alter the law or deviate from it, being a power to solve the community's practical problems, is a social good. The democratic principle is an answer to the question who should possess this good. According to this principle, it should be distributed equally among all members of the community. When someone breaks the law, he or she accordingly takes themselves a larger part than others have in the solution of the community's practical problems. I think this is what is meant when one who disobeys the law in a democracy is said to assume "greater say than others have about what should be done."[41] Disobeying laws in a democracy automatically means a breach of the democratic principle, that of equal distribution of the community's normative powers.

However, this explanation of the argument from fairness in a democracy, and of the manner in which the law is conceived of by this argument, carries the seeds of the limitations of this argument's conclusions. The law is perceived here as representing the community's normative state of affairs, but it obviously, in the context of the present argument, cannot be perceived as the sole representative of this state of affairs. The very context of the argument from democracy presupposes several meta-legal components of this state of affairs; the democratic principle itself and, through it, the theory of political and social justice of which this principle is merely one of many implications. If the equal distribution of goods is of moral value, then this value cannot be restricted to the social good of political power.

The very presuppositions of the present argument for obedience to the law, then, imply that the community's normative state of affairs comprises two parts. The first is meta-legal. It includes the set of principles composing the theory of social and political justice of which the democratic principle is one item only. The second part

---

True, the present majority has the power to change the current law and to enact new laws, but in practice this cannot be done immediately or all at once. The duty to obey the law, including the special duty to obey it in democracies, is a duty to obey it even if it isn't supported by the present majority. It isn't a duty to obey the wishes of the present majority before these have been given legal expression.

[41] Singer, *Democracy and Disobedience*, p. 36.

includes the set of rules composing the law. From the viewpoint of the democratic principle and that of the political theory of which it is a part, the power to change the community's normative state of affairs cannot extend to those areas of this state of affairs which are settled directly by this theory. Should the theory allow changes in the areas which it settles itself, it would be allowing internal contradictions resulting from its instructions. In other words, from the viewpoint of the political theory presupposed by the present argument for the duty to obey, i.e. the argument from the fairness of democracy, laws that settle matters already settled by the theory are void *ab initio*. They are *ultra vires* from the democratic point of view. The present argument for obedience accordingly applies only to matters on which the political theory of justice is neutral.

Several points must now be underlined. First, the argument just completed has no bearing whatsoever upon legal validity. In saying that laws settling matters already settled directly by the political theory are *ultra vires*, I do not mean that they are legally *ultra vires*. Their legal validity depends on the resolution of the dispute between theories of law, a dispute depending upon questions having to do with the nature of law, and not with the presuppositions of the argument for obedience based upon democracy. Moreover, the present argument is not only silent on the question of legal validity, it also supplies an only partial answer to the question of laws' moral validity. It only concerns the scope of the obedience that can be derived from the fairness of democracy. As there are other arguments grounding the moral duty to obey the law, such as the argument from negative consequences or the general fairness argument, it may be that laws the obedience to which is not supported by the argument from democracy will be given such support by the other arguments. In other words, it doesn't follow from the present argument that there is no moral duty to obey unjust laws. What follows from it is only that the argument from democracy cannot serve as grounds for such a duty, and consequently, that the duty to obey unjust laws in a democracy, is, if it exists, a far weaker duty there than the one to obey laws that are considered bad in aspects other than their justness. The first are only supported by the general arguments for obedience, those based on the negative consequences of disobedience, on the unfairness of unequal distribution of the burdens to be borne in order to prevent these consequences, on the duty to support just institutions and on communal obligation. The latter are also supported by the argument discussed here, based on the fairness of democracy. Unlike the general arguments, this last one ascribes more than merely instrumental value to obedience. It ascribes intrinsic value to it.

The distinction between these arguments and the distinction between their characters and scopes of application may supply more solid grounds for, and clarify, more than a few opinions voiced by philosophers on related and similar matters. I shall demonstrate with Dworkin's distinction between civil disobedience based on considerations of justice and civil disobedience based on considerations of policy, and with Singer's explanation of minorities' right to disobey.[42]

Dworkin suggested the distinction between justice-based civil disobedience and policy-based civil disobedience, in the article, "Civil Disobedience and Nuclear Protest."[43] It cites many Americans' disobedience to laws discriminating against blacks, or to the draft laws that sent them to fight in Vietnam, as examples of the former type of civil disobedience. The disobedience of numerous Europeans with regard to the deployment of American missiles in Europe is cited as an example of the second type of civil disobedience. Dworkin believes that every kind of civil disobedience requires justification, but he supports a lenient attitude towards the disobedience relating to considerations of justice, and not towards the disobedience relating to considerations of policy. He does so as he considers the first type consistent with the foundations of democracy. This is not the case regarding the second type, when it is not performed for the purpose of persuading the majority that its policy is wrong, but in order to force it to change this policy.

The analysis offered above amounts to a more radical formulation of these views and it further illuminates their foundations, that is, the different reasons for obeying the law in democracies. According to this analysis, what Dworkin calls justice-based civil disobedience is in need of no justification from the viewpoint of the democratic grounds for obedience. It only needs justification from the viewpoint of the general grounds for obedience. This is not the case with policy-based civil disobedience. In my terms, this is a disobedience aimed against laws and policies on which justice is neutral. The demand of these laws and policies for obedience is supported not only by the general and instrumental reasons for obedience, but also by the non-instrumental reason for obedience, based on the fairness of democ-

---

[42] This analysis is also suited to Rawls' discussion of the limitations of the principle of participation and majority rule. See *A Theory of Justice*, pp. 356–62.
[43] See Dworkin, *A Matter of Principle*, p. 104.

racy. Ergo the liberal attitude which Dworkin rightly advocates towards justice-based civil disobedience on the one hand, and his almost complete rejection of the policy-based civil disobedience meant to achieve a change by force, on the other.

Singer claims that if "over a period of time...decisions are taken which put [a minority] at a disadvantage...surely...this makes the decision-procedure no more than a travesty of a fair compromise."[44] He consequently concludes that "members...who are treated unfairly have less reason for obeying the decision-procedure...than they would if they were treated fairly."[45] Later, he goes on to discuss the question of the number of unfair decisions necessary in order that the system be considered unfair. There is much truth in what Singer is saying here, but there are also many difficulties and much confusion. Why is it only those who are treated unfairly that have slimmer grounds for obeying the results of decision procedures? Why is it necessary that they be treated unfairly for some amount of time in order for the grounds for obedience to dwindle? Why say that the unfair results of the decision procedure only weaken the grounds for obedience, rather than annulling them altogether?

These questions may be unraveled if we return to the distinction between the reason for obedience based on the fairness of democracy, that is, the principle that one should not take more than a share of political power that equals those held by others, and the general reasons for obedience related to the need for preserving the law as a tool for determining and enforcing desirable conducts. As the first reason applies only to laws solving practical matters that are not settled directly by the theory of justice itself, laws discriminating against minorities are, from the viewpoint of this reason, altogether non-binding. This is true from the very moment of such laws' enactment. As the other grounds for obedience apply, on the one hand, to all laws including unjust ones, but only within a political–legal system which is moral as a whole, and because, on the other hand, one unjust law doesn't necessarily make the entire system immoral, the effect of such a law on the general grounds for obedience is merely to weaken them. It cannot automatically disqualify the value that consists of the preservation of this political system and of equal distribution of the burdens of its preservation. There must thus be additional unjust laws for the force of these grounds for obedience to succumb completely.

---

[44] Singer, *Democracy and Disobedience*, p. 42.   [45] *Ibid.*, p. 43.

Before proceeding to the second special argument for obedience arising from democracy, the argument based on the character of the democratic procedure, I will again stress the following point. The argument based on the fairness of democracy, presently under discussion, must be carefully distinguished from the general argument from fairness. Though both are arguments from fairness, they have to do with fairness in the distribution of very different goods, and different conclusions follow from each as regards obedience to the law. Fairness in the context of the democratic argument turns on the good of political power. The focal point of the general fairness argument is the good of being freed of the burdens required for the preservation of the law as a tool. While the first argument doesn't apply, in any way, to unjust laws, only to laws that are democratically valid, the second, when it applies to a given political system, may also apply to unjust laws. For if disobedience to unjust laws may cause undesirable consequences, then the burden of preventing such consequences must be shared equally among the members of the community.

Participation and consent

Unlike the former argument which turned on the very substance of democracy, on the claim that it constitutes a fair distribution of the power of decision throughout the community, the present argument has to do with the procedure through which this distribution is implemented, and the fact that people participate in this procedure. Some have claimed that such participation indicates something similar to consent, and that it accordingly generates an obligation to act in keeping with the procedure's results, that is, according to the law.

The nature of what it is that is similar to consent that voting in elections indicates has mainly been understood by theorists in two manners. According to one view, voting indicates *actual though indirect* consent. According to the second, voting should not be seen as indicating actual consent, but it should be seen *as if it were consent.* This is so as it creates the expectation that those who perform the act of voting will behave in keeping with its results, and because people must be held responsible for the reasonable expectations that they arouse, if others have relied on these.

The first view is posited by John Plamenatz, who terms this form of consent "indirect consent."[46] The second is offered by Peter Singer, who terms this type "quasi-consent," and relates it to the legal institution of estoppel by representation.[47] Singer reaches this view after joining some of Plamenatz's critics who point out the falsity of the assumption that people who vote in democratic elections agree, in practice, to behave in keeping with their outcome. "Lenin, for instance," he says, "regarded capitalist democracy as a mere cloak for capitalist rule, but he urged Communists to 'utilize reactionary parliaments in a truly revolutionary way,' so as to hasten revolution."[48] Singer believes his conception of the link between voting and consent, a conception that doesn't assume actual consent, to be free, due to this, of the faults attacked by Plamenatz's critics. Nonetheless, objections similar to the ones advanced against Plamenatz were also aimed against Singer.[49]

My impression is that inasmuch as the phenomenon of manifest non-democrats' participation in elections is supposed to endanger the thesis that these non-democrats themselves are not bound by the outcome of the vote, it may indeed succeed in doing so. This is so whether the thesis of the obligation undertaken through voting in elections is based on estoppel or on actual consent. However, the phenomenon of manifest non-democrats poses no danger whatsoever to this thesis in the context of those who are not non-democrats. This is so as the meaning of a practice (on which the conception of voting as consent is based) and, usually, also the reasonableness of the expectations arising from acts of participating in the practice (on which the conception of estoppel-based account is grounded), bear no relation to the subjective mental state of some of the participants in the practice. They're related to the point of the practice and the expectations regarding it, harbored by most of its participants.

Just as there are manifest non-democrats who vote, and people know this, there are liars who use speech and insincere promisors who make promises, and people know this. All this shows is that the fact that people speak or make promises suggests that when people speak and promise, not all of them are in the mental state of telling the truth or meaning to keep their promises. It doesn't show that speech or promises should not be conceived of as acts which bind their performers to speaking the truth or keeping promises, respectively.

---

[46] See John Plamenatz, *Man and Society* (London: Longman, 1963), pp. 239–40.
[47] See Singer, *Democracy and Disobedience*, pp. 47–53.   [48] *Ibid.*, p. 53.
[49] See Raz, *The Authority of Law*, p. 242.

For the creation of these duties doesn't depend on a mental state that suits the acts of speech and promising. It depends on the justification for the general practice of which these acts are part, and on the performance of these acts. As the objective of the practice of voting (and this, it seems, is implicit in either Singer's or Plamenatz's explanation) is to reach practical solutions to public problems or to elect a body which will do so, those who are manifest non-democrats, and vote in the elections, rightly arouse expectations that they will act in keeping with these solutions.

The question whether the manifest non-democrats bind themselves to the outcome of the vote through their act of voting is a more complex one. My doubt on this matter turns on the question whether their act of voting should be perceived as analogous to the case where someone says, "I promise to do such and such, but I have no intention of keeping this promise," or to cases of promises made by people generally known not to keep their promises, promises made by Smiths to Browns, when the Smiths tell the Millers, but not the Browns, that they have no intentions of keeping these promises, etc. The first case is that of the speaker who doesn't bind himself or herself in promising. He or she presents the addressee with a self-contradictory statement which thus counts as saying nothing. In the second type of case, the speakers are bound by virtue of their utterances. What decides the question of the creation of an obligation in both these cases is the question whether the addressee is justified in perceiving them as promises. The actual intentions of the speaker are not the decisive factor, for these intentions are identical in both cases. My impression is that the case of non-democrats, at least when they don't declare themselves as such at the polls and upon voting, is closer to the second type of case listed above. They should be seen as binding themselves by voting. If they declare themselves to be non-democrats upon voting, they shouldn't be seen as binding themselves. However, then their votes should also be excluded from the general count determining the elections' outcome.

It should be noted that the question whether manifest non-democrats are duty-bound by their act of voting is not of much practical significance. It has to do with a marginal portion of the scope to which an anyway non-universal argument applies. Perhaps this comment should end my discussion of the argument from participation: it is a secondary and partial argument relative to the one based on democracy's fairness. If the latter succeeds, then it succeeds in showing that everyone who has received his or her portion of the political power is duty-bound to obey the law, whether he or she has used this power or not. The argument from participation in elections holds only for those who have actually exercised the political power granted them, that is, it holds only for those who have actively participated in the democratic procedure.

CHAPTER 4

The limits of the duty to obey the law

The first part of the previous chapter dealt with the question of the conditions that a political system must meet in order for the duty to obey to apply to its laws. However, as we already know, the fact that a political system meets these conditions and that the duty to obey indeed applies to its laws doesn't mean that this duty dictates obedience every time it applies, or under any circumstances. The duty to obey the law is not, and cannot be, an absolute duty. It is a duty that may sometimes be overriden by other moral considerations. What are these considerations? What weight do they carry relative to that of the duty to obey the law? These are the questions that will occupy the present chapter. My answers to them will form a theory of the limits of the duty to obey.

I cannot offer complete answers to the two questions posed above. A full answer to the first question, i.e. which considerations justify disobedience, depends on the answer to yet another question: which value system should one adopt. An attempt to reply to this last question goes far beyond the scope of this book. Here, I shall point out the considerations that justify disobedience, so far as these follow from the inner logic of the foundations of the duty to obey discussed by the previous chapters. This inner logic will also form the basis for my answer to the second question concerning the limits of the duty to obey, the question of how to assess the force of this duty, relative to other values.

I will begin by examining the limits of obedience from the point of view of a citizen who asks him or herself whether or not it is justified to disobey. I shall then discuss this question from the point of view of authorities and citizens who ask themselves how to deal with the disobedient. Many of us tend to think of the limits of obedience without distinguishing between the two. This confusion is almost identical to the confusion mentioned in the first chapter, between the duty to obey the law and the value of the rule of law. It causes optical illusions which in turn lead to many practical mistakes. Many abstain from disobeying the law despite the fact that such disobedience is justified, as they adopt the authorities' point of view. Conversely, many show intolerance towards the authorities when these are intolerant of disobedience, either in cases when it is justified or in those when it is not. It is worthwhile trying to prevent this confusion. An answer to the question of the justified attitude towards disobedience cannot be derived automatically from an answer to the question of the justification of actual acts of disobedience. On the one hand, an act of disobedience may be justified, while tolerance towards it is unjustified. On the other hand, an act of disobedience may be unjustified, while tolerance towards it is justified. The first possibility arises from considerations of the separation of powers. As I clarified in the first chapter, the considerations based on justifying obedience to the law carry much more weight at a junction where the authorities are active. Consequently, the authorities aren't justified in tolerating every action whose performance is justified at the junction where the citizen is active.[1] The second possibility arises, for the most part, from considerations of freedom of conscience. Despite the fact that a political morality may not justify disobedience, it can justify tolerance of disobedience undertaken on the basis of such considerations. Accordingly, the question that should be answered first is that of the limits of obedience from the citizen's point of view. Only then will I deal with these limits from the authorities' point of view, i.e. with the question of when the authorities are justified in intolerance of justified (as well as unjustified) disobedience, and when they are justified in tolerating unjustified (as well as justified) disobedience.

I. JUSTIFYING DISOBEDIENCE

The argument from consequences: the formal limits of obedience and the complex criterion for disobedience

The various foundations of the duty to obey defended in the previous chapters differ in their inner logic. They also differ as to the conceptions of law that they presuppose and in the evaluative

---

[1] See also section 1 of the first chapter, pp. 6–7 above.

assumptions implicit in each. Subsequently, the limits of the duty to obey following from these various bases are not strictly identical. I shall begin with the limits following from the argument from consequences. According to this argument, we must obey laws so as to preserve the effectivity of law as a mechanism for instituting and enforcing desirable conducts.[2] This argument presupposes the existence of an answer to the question: which are the desirable conducts? But (as I shall show later), unlike the other arguments, it contains no intimations, slight or otherwise, as to the contents of this answer. To answer this question, we must turn to those values of political morality which we should hold. What, precisely, is this morality? This matter, as stated, goes far beyond the limits of the present discussion. However, the argument from consequences makes it possible to determine formal limits for the duty to obey, limits which will suit any political morality whatsoever, regardless of its contents.

In terms of the argument from consequences, any political morality whatsoever will justify and require only *limited obedience* which is carefully considered relative to the laws pertaining to matters settled by the morality itself. It will justify and require massive and *nearly absolute obedience* to laws settling matters on which the morality itself

---

[2] On this argument see chapter 2, above, pp. 66–78. Perhaps it should be noted here that the practical role of the theory of the limits of the duty to obey the law is more than supplying normative guidance, a role fulfilled by theories on the limits of other moral duties as well. The public presence of a theory on the limits of the duty to obey plays a role in decreasing, somewhat, the danger posed by disobedience to the law's effectivity as a tool for enforcing and instituting social conducts. Such cases of disobedience endanger this effectivity for they may be understood to be denials of the law's authority as an institution determining these conducts. Its success as such a tool depends, to a large extent, on the secure belief of most of its subjects that most of its subjects are indeed prepared to, or will in fact, perform the law's instructions. (If I am willing to follow the law's instructions in order to allow it to be the institution determining conducts in society, but I don't know whether the majority will follow these instructions, there is no point in implementing my willingness to follow the instructions. If the majority doesn't follow them, the law will not be the institution which determines social conducts.) The existence of such a secure belief is mainly dependent upon the fact that the majority of the law's subjects do indeed follow its instructions. However, it also depends on two other factors: on the way in which the authorities respond to disobedience to the law, and on the meanings ascribed by the law's subjects to acts of disobedience on the part of other subjects: do these acts express denial of the law's power to determine conducts in society, and if so to what extent? If the limits of this power of the law's are delineated and known beforehand – a state which should be advanced by a theory on the limits of the duty to obey – disobedience to laws that fall outside of the scope to which this duty applies will not be understood as denials of the law's power to determine the conducts of society. They will not endanger the law's operation in determining conducts in the boundaries within which the duty to obey applies.

gives no definitive instructions.[3] Later, I shall formulate both these theses, that of limited obedience and that of nearly absolute obedience, in a more detailed and meticulous manner. What they mean is that on matters of morality (matters settled by morality), the duty to obey the law is limited almost exclusively to areas in which the directives of morality are ambiguous, and that the essence of the moral duty to obey the law has to do with amoral matters, matters on which morality is neutral.[4] Both the theses derive from the fact that the law, from the standpoint of any political morality regardless of its contents, is merely designed to enforce the values of this morality, and to settle matters on which it is indeterminate. Political moralities deal, by definition, with the very matters which occupy legal systems: they deal with the appropriate ways of organizing society, with its conduct and the conduct of the individuals within it. This along with the very question whether or not a duty to obey exists presupposes the logical and normative precedence of such moralities to the law (otherwise, what need would there be for a moral confirmation of the duty to obey the law?), and thus leads directly to the question, why should such a morality acknowledge the duty to obey the law? The answer lies in the fact that a political morality needs the institution of law, in order to enforce its values and principles and determine conduct in areas on which it is indeterminate. Disobedience endangers the effectivity of this institution in fulfilling these two roles.[5] The limited obedience thesis and the nearly absolute obedience thesis both follow from these truths.

Any and every political morality needs the law to enforce the conducts whose desirability is indicated by the given morality, due to certain truisms concerning human nature. There are some who lack the wisdom needed to recognize the morality's values. Most, however, are not possessed of the strength of character that would allow them sufficiently frequent action on these values. Most people know that taking bribes, assaulting, robbing and rape are prohibited. Unfortunately though, not all people know this. And many of those who do fail, at least at times, to overcome their drives in order to practice

---

[3] In speaking of a political morality, I am referring to any theory consisting of principles and values regarding society's conduct and the conduct of individuals within the social framework. In this sense religions which include instructions on such matters are also political moralities.

[4] For a similar view, arising from different reasons, see C. L. Carr, "The Problem of Political Authority," *Monist* 66 (1983), 472 especially from p. 482 onward.

[5] See chapter 2, above, pp. 71–4.

these bans. The law's punishment mechanism allows it to overcome the consequences of these human faults, to some extent. Thomas Hobbes gave this matter detailed, philosophical expression.

Any and every political morality needs the law as a tool for the institution of conduct arrangements, due to various facts about the nature of political moralities. These latter are not completely determinate. They do not contain views on every practical matter that arises in community life, and the views that they do contain on some matters are somewhat vague. Political moralities do not contain answers to questions such as the economic favorability of developing a given fighter jet rather than its alternatives, or on the favorability of driving on the left rather than the right side of the road. They have positions on the question whether income tax should be high or low, but they don't have clear-cut stances on the question whether low income tax means twenty or twenty-one percent. Someone must decide these matters.[6] Here, the law has the role of instituting the desirable conducts, and not only the role of urging the actualization of conducts thought to be desirable independently of the law.[7] Thomas Aquinas says similar things of the role of human law with regard to natural law.

The limited obedience thesis follows from the fact that in matters on which a political morality is determinate, by virtue of their very definition as such, the law's role can be nothing other than enforcement. As these are morally determinate areas, there is no need here for the law to create new principles of conduct. Here it should only express the principles considered valid in the first place, for instance, that the innocent shouldn't be punished, or that civil servants should not be bribed, or that freedom of expression should not be infringed upon (if liberalism is the correct political morality), or that territories should not be evacuated in the interests of peace (if nationalism is the correct political morality). If the law nonetheless takes the trouble to determine instructions on these matters, and these differ from those of the political morality, then the law is

---

[6] For additional examples, pertinent to the core of criminal law, see W. S. Boardman, "Coordination and the Moral Obligation to Obey the Law," *Ethics* 97 (1987), 546 especially pp. 548, 551–2. See also my article "The Normativity of Law and its Co-ordinative Function," *Israel Law Review* 16 (1981), 333.

[7] Anarchist social theories will require the institution of law, but not for the enforcement of values, as such theories are based on a belief in the possibility of reforming man's evil nature. However, they will require the institution of law for purposes of legislating on practical matters and for purposes of deciding practical disputes that aren't settled or decided by moral and political values.

overstepping its role as enforcer of this morality. Moreover, this means that the law is actually doing the opposite of enforcing the morality. The reasons due to which the latter may nevertheless prescribe obedience to laws which contradict its values have to do with the possibility that disobeying these laws will endanger the law's effectivity as an institution which generally serves the morality's values. The question whether these reasons are indeed decisive in a concrete situation depends on the balance between two sets of variables. On the one hand, it depends on the intensity of the damage to the functioning of the legal system by the disobedience, modified by the factor of the level of enforcement that the system supplies the political morality and the probability that such damage will occur. On the other hand, it depends on the intensity of the damage facing the value due to which the law is objectionable, modified by the factor of this value's importance and the probability that such damage will occur. This is the detailed formation of the thesis of limited obedience.

It is important to note here that when the laws in question damage the areas in which the principles or values of a given political morality reign absolute, then it is clear that the political morality will justify and even demand disobedience to these laws.[8] This will be the case, for instance, when the laws ordain injury to innocent people in the interests of enlarging national territories, in the context of a humanist political morality, or when the laws ordain abandonment of lands in the interests of peace, in the context of a fascist morality.

In contrast to the limited obedience that the political morality will justify regarding matters on which this morality itself has instructions, it will demand and justify nearly absolute obedience regarding matters on which it does not. The logic of this thesis is identical to that of the limited obedience thesis. For matters on which the political morality is indeterminate, the law's instructions cannot, according to this assumption, damage the values of this morality. Allowing disobedience in such cases means allowing damage to an institution advancing the realization of the morality's values, in an area where, *ex hypothesi*, the law cannot damage these values. A political morality,

---

[8] In speaking of the absolute dominance of principles I'm referring to what I discussed above with regard to duties' areas of absolute control. On this matter see chapter 1, above, pp. 18–19. It is also worth noting that not every political theory will necessarily be formulated in terms of principles and duties with areas of absolute dominance. Some political theories may, naturally, be formulated in purely consequentialist terms. Of course, for such theories, the claims in this chapter to which this footnote pertains, do not apply.

regardless of its contents, will accordingly hesitate to allow disobedience of this type. When someone opposes a decision to terminate a given strategic project, which she sees as mistaken in terms of economic efficiency, and cannot tie her opposition to the values of the political morality to which she adheres in a manner clearly ruling out the project's termination, she will not be able to enlist the support of this political morality for her desire to disobey the government's decisions on the project. This is so as the law's role with regard to the political morality is to enforce its values. If disobeying laws undermines the law's effectivity in fulfilling this role, and if the political morality lacks a clear-cut position on the matter of opposition to decisions regarding the strategic project in question, how can this morality permit a breach of the duty to obey that is intended to express such opposition?

Despite all this, the fact that the duty to obey is almost absolute in the context of laws bearing upon matters where the political morality is indeterminate does not imply that these laws may never be disobeyed. Two things should be kept in mind as regards this issue. First, the duty to obey is not only, as we already know, not absolute, it is also not universal. It is a duty the justifications of which do not necessarily apply to each and every situation to which laws do.[9] Laws and applications of laws pertaining to matters on which the political morality lacks its own instructions may sometimes be such that the justifications for the duty to obey do not apply in their cases. For instance, in the case of foolish laws whose folly is generally acknowledged, and which are disobeyed on these grounds, disobedience will almost certainly not count as an expression of unfairness towards the legal system's other subjects. The disobeyer will act on a willingness to allow everyone to disobey under the same circumstances. (In other words, he will allow anyone to disobey when the laws are foolish, are generally recognized as such, and are generally known to be disobeyed on these grounds.) Such general disobedience will furthermore cause no damaging consequences. It will damage neither the good produced by the laws in question, as these are, *ex hypothesi*, foolish laws, producing no good, nor the functioning of the institution of law in producing useful goods or in settling disputes. This is so as, according to our assumptions, the laws in question produce no useful goods and this fact is unanimously agreed upon. Second, even in cases where the duty to obey applies

---

[9] See chapter 2, above, pp. 73–8.

and demands obedience to laws settling matters on which the political morality is silent, exemptions from its demand may nonetheless be granted at times. As we shall see in the second part of this chapter, a political morality may show tolerance towards disobedience which is based on values contradicting its own. It will not justify such disobedience, but may nonetheless allow it. If this is the case regarding values which contradict its own, then, given the same circumstances (to be discussed in detail below),[10] it must certainly be the case with regard to disobedience based on values towards which it is neutral.

Both the limited obedience thesis and the nearly absolute obedience thesis may be confirmed in terms of the concept of moral autonomy. As the first chapter shows, one gives up one's moral autonomy when one acts against the balance of moral reasons.[11] Accordingly, theories of political morality have no reason not to justify and to demand absolute obedience on matters as to which they are indeterminate. By the very fact of their moral indeterminacy, nearly absolute or even absolute obedience regarding them, doesn't amount to a willingness to give up deliberation or action on moral reasons. On the other hand, theories of political morality have every reason to prohibit absolute obedience on matters which are settled by their values. These values, by their very definition, make a willingness to give up action that is based on them, a willingness to give up action based on the balance of moral reasons. This, then, means a surrender of moral autonomy.

The values and intentions of the legislators and policy makers

Evaluations made in order to determine the data which is supposed to populate the sets of variables included in the limited obedience thesis must give special status to the intentions of the legislators or the policy makers. In referring to the level of enforcement which the legal system supplies the political morality, when considering the question of disobedience, we should not limit ourselves to the extent of the actual fit between the laws comprising the given legal system and the values of the morality. We should also include the probability that this level of enforcement will increase or decrease. This factor depends, to a large extent, upon the wills, intentions and talents of the current legislators and policy makers. If the policies against which the disobedience in question is directed were adopted

[10] See pp. 155–9 below.   [11] See pp. 10–11 and note 18, p. 17 above.

by the authorities in full view of the damage they would cause to moral values, or if they resulted from mistaken considerations which are likely to recur due to faulty characters, minds or moral stances on the part of the legislators, then this fact is reason enough to assume that the level of enforcement that this political–legal system supplies these values will gradually decrease. The situation is quite different when these policies were adopted due to a coincidental mistake in reasoning. When the policy of non-settlement in the West Bank is managed on the basis of a minimalist Zionist ideology, then the reasons that the fundamentalist right-wing movement, Gush Emunim, has to disobey the laws serving this policy are much weightier than they would be if the policy were based on considerations of political tactics stemming from a simple mistake. The same may be said of the assessment of the extent of damage that disobedience may cause the level of enforcement that the legal system supplies the political morality; so, too, of the assessment of the damage that obedience may cause to the value damaged by the law which is the candidate for disobedience. Disobedience may damage the level of enforcement that a legal system supplies the political morality, in the sense of the legal system's becoming a less efficient tool of enforcement. However, disobedience may also improve the level of enforcement that the legal system supplies the values of a given political morality by causing the legislators and policy makers not to depart from these values from now on, or to do so to a lesser extent. (If we hit the right hand of a criminal in the act, we may impair not only his or her ability to commit crimes, but also his or her ability to perform productive acts. The loss, however, may prove a gain – from here on he or she may perform only or more acts of the latter type.) As regards assessment of the damage which obedience may cause the value endangered by the law which is the candidate for disobedience, the legislators' intentions as well as additional details regarding them are, again, relevant. If they have purposely impaired this value, or impaired it due to a non-accidental mistake, it is likely that obeying the law will encourage them to continue damaging this value. Accordingly, the legislators' and policy makers' intentions as well as various other facts about them (for instance: how long the positions in question will be occupied by these people or by others who resemble them in the relevant aspects) should play central roles in determining the concrete values of the variables in the function for deciding the justifiability of disobedience to specific laws.

It is here, perhaps, that the obvious should be stressed: if it is possible to alter the law or policies endangering the values of the political morality in a lawful manner, then this line of action should clearly be preferred. This conclusion follows naturally from the limited obedience thesis. The limited obedience thesis stems from the tension between the direct threat posed by individual laws to the political morality's values, and the indirect threat under which disobedience to these laws places the values, impairing the effectivity of the legal system as a whole as a tool for enforcing values. If the first threat may be removed with no concurrent manifestation of the second, then it is obvious that this is what should be done. If the legal system itself supplies ways of preventing it from damaging the values that it is supposed to serve, then these ways should unquestionably be tried first. However, we should remember that the existence of a legal possibility for altering the law doesn't always mean the existence of real possibilities for its alteration. What counts with regard to the question whether or not to disobey a law endangering values that should be realized is not the legal possibility of changing the law but the actual possibility of changing it.[12] The question whether or not such a possibility exists depends, as stated, on the many and complex components of the political reality in question.

The formal limits of obedience and two simple criteria for disobedience

The fact that political realities are usually complex and highly complicated is one that makes it difficult to apply the thesis of limited obedience as it was formulated above, and to decide the question whether to obey or disobey laws contradicting the values of the political morality. This difficulty doesn't occur on the level of moral theory. As stated, it stems from the complexity of actual reality, from the open-ended fabric of future reality, and from our limited capability to know all of these in their entirety. Due to this, it is highly tempting to set simple and clear criteria for the justification of disobedience of the kind under discussion, criteria which will be independent of the assessment of such complex data. The central fear behind this wish to set criteria is the fear that in their absence, the wide border-zone between justified and unjustified disobedience will become a slippery slope under the footing of the law as enforcer of

---

[12] For a similar view see Greenawalt, *Conflicts of Law and Morality*, p. 229.

desirable conducts, sliding us straight down to anarchy. Some, accordingly, see the only cases in which disobeying the law is justified as those where it orders actions which are blatantly opposed to the political morality, or blatantly damage its values.[13] The fear motivating the determination of such criteria is not altogether groundless. However, it isn't reason enough for abandoning the complex criterion for justifying disobedience. This is so for two reasons. First, the slippery slope created by the complex criterion is two-wayed. If the criterion's complexity and its open link with the fabric of actual life and reality allow for a possible slide from justified to unjustified disobedience, they also allow for a slide from justified to unjustified obedience. The first slide endangers the law's effectivity. The second one endangers people's moral integrity. In view of this latter danger a simple criterion opposing the first should be determined, i.e. that it is justified to disobey laws that damage the values of morality, whenever the extent of this damage is slightly more than marginal. Second, adopting the simple criterion meant to protect the legal system means giving the legislators and policy makers moral guarantees that they will enjoy the cooperation of the law's subjects upon initiating acts that damage the morality slightly less than blatantly. Morally bad laws and policies are morally bad even when they aren't blatantly so. And they are products of human action. If the law's creators have moral guarantees that only blatantly immoral laws will be disobeyed, they may be tempted to misuse their authority to enact slightly less than blatantly immoral laws, or to exploit the laws in the interests of similarly immoral policies. The vague situation created by a complex criterion which is open to reality's indeterminacy and complexity may help counteract such a temptation. If we wish to replace this criterion with a simpler one, it would seem that the two arguments just presented support the simple criterion opposing the one that is usually advocated. In other words, what they support is not the view that it is justified to disobey laws only when they blatantly violate moral values, but the view that it is justified to disobey all the laws whose damage to these values is more than very slight.

This last conclusion will probably be opposed by some who will claim that its acceptance empties the moral duty to obey the law of all practical content. If this duty supports only the performance of the

---

[13] The criteria set by Rawls (*A Theory of Justice*, pp. 371–7) for justifying the performance of civil disobedience are an example of such criteria. See also Boardman, "Coordination and the Moral Obligation to Obey the Law," pp. 555–6.

actions commanded by laws whose degree of moral badness is slight, it very nearly becomes redundant.[14] This is so as actions that are ordained by laws that are good from the point of view of the political morality are actions that should be performed not only because of the duty to obey the law, but because they are morally good.[15] And if the duty to obey the law supports only the performance of actions ordained by laws whose degree of moral badness is minimal, this makes it an unimportant duty. Before replying to this objection, I would like to comment that I'm not making a decisive claim to the effect that the borderline of obedience to laws contradicting the political morality should run along the set of slight infringements upon these values. Adopting the open and complex criterion for disobedience, according to which disobedience is decided by the balance between the damage caused by disobedience and that caused by obedience, may supply an adequate answer to the problem of possible misuse of authority on the part of legislators and policy makers. Adherence to this criterion is also capable of providing a suitable balance between the twin slippery slopes which it creates. The question whether to adopt this complex criterion or one of the simple ones may be answered differently in different societies, according to the assessment of their members' moral maturity, and according to the nature of the people who tend to deal with legislating and policy making in each society. I won't elaborate any further on this point. It is, however, important to see that even if one adopts the simple criterion according to which the duty to obey the law only supports the performance of actions whose degree of moral badness is minimal, this does not make it an unimportant duty. Many laws institute conduct on matters with regard to which a political morality is indeterminate. Many people may object to the contents of these laws as they contradict their personal or sectorial interests or further goals or means that are objectionable on the basis of practical views which are not part of the political morality (for example, aesthetic views as regards planning laws, strategic views as regards defense policies, etc.). The duty to obey the law is of considerable practical importance due to the fact that these laws exist, as the thesis of nearly absolute obedience applies in just this context. When objections to such laws originate in practical views that are not part

---

[14] A similar argument is discussed above with regard to the grounding of the duty to obey on the negative consequences that disobedience to laws may cause. See chapter 2, section 4, pp. 70–1 above.   [15] See chapter 2, p. 71 and chapter 3, pp. 104–5 above.

of the political morality, they can hardly justify a departure from the duty to obey.[16]

Democracy, fairness and communal obligation: substantive limits of obedience

Both of the theses of the limits of obedience which I have tried to support so far, the thesis of limited obedience and that of nearly absolute obedience, are founded on the argument from negative consequences. The political morality that should be adhered to determines which consequences are considered negative. Situations which fascism would consider negative would be considered positive by liberalism and vice versa. The limits of obedience following from the argument from consequences are thus totally formal. At least three of the additional arguments supporting the duty to obey the law – the argument from fairness,[17] the argument from the nature of democracy,[18] and that based on communal obligation[19] – may aid us in imbuing these formal boundaries with substance, or at least partially so.

Unlike the argument from consequences, these arguments presuppose more than *the mere existence of a political morality*, enjoying precedence to the law. They also imply at least part of *the contents of this morality*. The validity of the general fairness argument and the argument from fairness in a democracy depends on a political morality the core of which is a humanistic conception of justice. In other words, it presupposes a conception of justice that turns on the equal value of human beings. Were this central principle not presupposed, what importance would there be to the equal distribution of the burdens required for the maintenance of the institution of law? Were its validity not assumed, why should it be at all important to distribute the power of political decision-making equally throughout society? The validity of the argument from communal obligation stems from the existence of ideals and interests that are unique to the community to which these obligations are owed. Were the existence of such unique ideals and interests not presupposed, and were it not supposed that they merited special service, what importance could we attach to these communal obligations?

---

[16] However, see pp. 126–7 above (my discussion of the qualification of the thesis of nearly absolute obedience).   [17] Chapter 2, above, pp. 57–66.

[18] Chapter 3, above, pp. 109–16.   [19] Chapter 2, above, pp. 83–9.

Whoever adheres to the duty to obey the law on the basis of more than just the argument from negative consequences, adopting one or more of the three additional foundations, is possessed of an answer that exceeds the question of how to measure the force of the duty to obey the law against other values with which it clashes. Such people have at least partial answers to the question about what the values are whose impairment requires such an act of measuring. These are the values having to do with human beings' equal value and with the ideals and the interests of the community towards which the duty to obey is especially owed. If any laws damage these values and ideals, then in accordance with the standards for measuring the weight of the duty to obey stemming from the consequence argument, the thesis of limited obedience applies to these laws. If these laws endanger human beings' equal value in such a manner that disobeying them will further this value more than obeying them, then they should be disobeyed. If they endanger communal ideals and interests in such a manner that disobeying them will further these ideals and interests more than obeying them, then they should be disobeyed. (In accordance with the standards for measuring the weight of the duty to obey following from the democratic argument, these laws aren't even worthy of limited obedience. They reside, as shown by the previous chapter, outside the scope of the duty to obey the law stemming from the democratic argument.[20])

The democratic argument, the argument from fairness and the argument from communal obligation, all add roots to the duty to obey the law and, as I have just explained, make it possible to assign substance to its formal boundaries, as these are outlined by the consequence argument. It is very important to see that neither the branching out of the duty's roots nor their imbuement with substance means any extension in the circumference of its limits. The three arguments justify and require nearly absolute obedience to laws dealing with matters that are not determined by the values from which these arguments derive – from humanistic values when dealing with the argument from fairness or democracy, and from communal ideals and interests when dealing with the argument from communal obligation. The democratic argument, as demonstrated in the previous chapter, doesn't to any extent prescribe obedience to laws that damage the values of humanistic morality, not even limited

[20] See chapter 3, above, pp. 112–13.

obedience. The fairness argument is subordinate to the concept of law implied by the argument from consequences, i.e. to a conception of it as a tool for the enforcement and institution of worthwhile conducts, and to the conception of disobedience as an action capable of damaging this tool. This argument accordingly prescribes only limited obedience to laws which damage humanistic values.[21] The argument from communal obligations is subordinate, as an argument for the duty to obey the law, to the conception of law implied by the argument from consequences.[22] It thus prescribes only limited obedience to laws that damage communal ideals and interests. Subsequently, for someone who adheres to the duty to obey the law due to all or any of these arguments, and not due to the argument from consequences alone, this duty will grow in muscularity rather than corpulence.

Communal ideals and interests on the one hand, and the values having to do with humans' equal value on the other, may fail to coincide. They may indeed clash. Laws and policies may serve communal ideals and interests while damaging the values of humanistic justice. Conversely, they may serve the values of humanistic justice, while damaging communal ideals and interests. The solution of such clashes, from the point of view of humanistic theories of justice is of the type indicated by Dworkin.[23] Such theories of justice do not reject communal ideals etc. or action in their interests, just as they do not reject personal ideals and interests or action that furthers these. However, they place limitations on these ideals and interests. For those who adhere to such ideals and interests under a humanistic theory of values, such clashes will be solved according to the limits of obedience following from the humanistic arguments. Laws and policies that damage the values of humanism on behalf of communal ideals and interests, will, at most, be assigned the limited obedience following from the argument from fairness. (According to the boundary lines following from the democratic argument they will, as stated, be situated completely outside the realm of obedience.) The limits of obedience following from the argument from communal obligation will only bind if they accord with the limits following from the humanistic arguments. The only

---

[21] See chapter 2 above, p. 61 (on the subordination of the argument from fairness to the argument from consequences), and chapter 3, above, pp. 113–16 (on the comparison between the limits following from the argument from democracy and the argument from fairness, and the clarification of Dworkin's and Singer's claims in this context).

[22] See chapter 2, above, pp. 87–9.   [23] See chapter 2, above, p. 85.

laws and policies that will be candidates for exclusion from the limits
of obedience following from the communal obligation argument will
be such that the reason due to which they fail to serve communal
ideals and interests with maximum efficiency is unrelated to the
values of humanistic justice.

I have dealt, so far, with the limits of obedience following from the
argument from consequences, the general argument from fairness,
the argument from fairness in a democracy and the argument from
communal obligation. The previous chapters defended two additional foundations for the duty to obey the law: one having to do
with the duty to support just institutions[24] and the other having to do
with participation in the democratic process.[25] These foundations
neither add to nor subtract from the matter of the limits of obedience
derived from the other arguments. The argument from the duty to
support just institutions may be conceived of, for our purposes, in two
ways. First, it may be viewed within the historical context in which
it was proposed: that of Rawls' theory of justice. As this is a
humanistic theory of justice, the limits of the duty to obey that follow
from this argument will be identical to those following from the
argument from fairness. Second, the argument may be abstracted
from its historical context. Any theory of justice, regardless of its
contents, and not just the one proposed by Rawls, must adopt a duty
to support institutions seen as just, according to its principles. Any
theory of justice must do this in order to achieve concretization. The
duty to support just institutions, when conceived of in this manner,
that is, in abstraction from Rawls' theory of justice or any specific
theory of justice, entails formal limits for the duty to obey the law,
which coincide exactly with those entailed by the argument from
consequences.

The argument based on participation in a democracy is a source of
limits identical to those derived from the argument from fairness
under democracy. If participation in democratic elections means
consent to obeying laws, there is no reason to see this as a consent to
obey laws that depart from whatever agrees with democracy's
essence. If participation in democratic elections should be seen either
as, or as if it were, an expression of consent, then it should be seen as
such only with regard to what democracy stands for. This consent,
then, is consent to obey only the laws settling matters which are not

[24] See chapter 2, above, pp. 78–83.   [25] See chapter 3, above, pp. 116–19.

determined by the political theory to which the democratic principle belongs.

What I have dealt with here are the limits of the duty to obey following from the foundations of this duty defended in the previous chapters. Some of these foundations presuppose humanism. Others do not. I have not, in this discussion, presented a case for humanism. It therefore doesn't follow from my present discussion that the duty to obey the law cannot be adopted exclusively on the basis of the argument from negative consequences, either with or without the argument from communal obligations, and totally independently of either the democratic argument or the argument from fairness. In other words, my description of the limits of the duty to obey in the context of its humanistic foundations is valid only for those who adhere to this duty due to these arguments, or in case the humanistic political morality is that which should be adhered to. The only theses on the duty to obey defended unconditionally here are those of limited obedience and nearly absolute obedience, theses both of which follow from the argument from consequences. This is an argument which must be held by anyone who holds any political morality whatsoever. (Someone who holds no such morality will have no interest at all in the question of the moral duty to obey the law.) As this argument is, as stated, valid under any political morality, whatever its contents, the limited obedience thesis and the nearly absolute obedience thesis are also valid under any political morality. However, the substance to be incorporated into these formal theses will change from one such morality to another.

Those who tried, in 1976, to enlist the aid of the duty to obey the law, to talk Gush Emunim (Israeli fundamentalists of the extreme right wing) out of settling near Kadum, a West Bank village, were consequently wasting their breath. If the duty was enlisted on the basis of its consequence-foundation, then their criticism was unjustified from the point of view of the political morality adhered to by Gush Emunim. The settlement at Kadum, situated in the heart of Samaria, was meant to serve and indeed succeeded in serving the value most central to this morality: the rule of the Jewish people in the biblical Land of Israel. If it was enlisted on the basis of the duty's humanistic foundations, the resulting arrows of criticism simply missed the target altogether. Disobedience at Kadum clearly fell outside the boundaries of the duty to obey following from the consequence argument, when these were imbued with the fundamental values of nationalistic political morality. This must be demonstrated in terms of a comparison. The extent of damage caused by the non-settlement policy to the value of keeping the fatherland intact, modified by the factor of the force possessed by this value in the context of Gush Emunim's political morality, must be compared to the extent of damage caused by the disobedience in question to the political–legal system which at that point was not, in any case, adequately furthering their morality. As to the humanistic foundations, Gush Emunim, in view of the principles of its nationalistic political morality, cannot adhere to a duty to obey the law based on these foundations. Criticizing the movement for failing to fulfill the duty to obey based on these principles is like criticizing a Catholic for eating non-Kosher food. Prior conversion would be advisable.

The current efforts of those who enlist the aid of the duty to obey in convincing objectors to military service in the West Bank and Gaza to abandon their stance are at the very most of temporary value. If the duty is enlisted on the basis of the argument from consequences, then these efforts are directed against an objection which almost definitely falls outside the limits of the duty following from this foundation. These formal limits should be imbued with the values adhered to by the objectors. The values they hold are humanistic. From the point of view of these values, disobeying is better than obeying in the case in question, either at the moment or in the immediately visible future. In order to see this, one must draw a comparison. The extent of the damage done by the continued and purposeful policy of dominating a foreign nation for nationalistic reasons, to the principle by which every person has a right to national self-determination, must be compared to the extent of the damage caused by such disobedience to the political–legal system which is, in any case, gradually ceasing to further humanistic values. All of this also applies to the limits following from the fairness argument, an argument which, as stated, is subordinate to the conception of law at the root of the consequence argument. If the duty to obey is enlisted on the basis of the democratic argument, then the efforts of dissuasion are definitely hopeless. They resemble a recourse to the duty to keep promises, to persuade a person who promised under duress to torture someone to keep this promise. As I have already stated, the democratic foundations of the duty to obey the law cannot apply at all to laws that impinge upon the principles of humanism. In short, Gush Emunim couldn't be persuaded by means of the fairness or the democratic argument for the duty to obey the law, as its members don't adhere to the duty on this basis. Conversely, it's difficult to persuade those presently considering objection to serve in the occupied territories by means of these arguments, precisely because they do adhere to the duty to obey based on these grounds.

Justifying civil disobedience and conscientious objection

The last twenty-five years have witnessed important discussions of political disobedience in the context of the distinction between civil disobedience and conscientious objection. These two types of disobedience differ, chiefly, as to the goals that their performers intend to attain by using them. Civil disobedience is disobedience intended to attain a change in the policy or the principle served or expressed by the law being disobeyed or by another law.[26] Conscientious objection is disobedience of more modest intent: that of saving the disobeyer's conscience.[27] There is no point in answering

[26] See, for instance, Rawls, *A Theory of Justice*, p. 364. There are many other components of Rawls' definition of civil disobedience. Some of these have been criticized. On this matter see Raz, *The Authority of Law*, chs. 14, 15, and also Greenawalt, *Conflicts of Law and Morality*, pp. 232–3. Another component worth comment here has to do with the exclusion of disobedience to a law due to personal or sectorial interests, from the realm of civil disobedience. By virtue of what has been said above on the justification of disobedience to laws on the basis of inclusive objections, such interested disobedience will not be justified according to most of the prevalent political moralities. For most political moralities do not define considerations of personal or sectorial interests as their considerations. However, I'm not sure that Rawls is right in excluding interested disobedience from the very concept of "civil disobedience." Though there is a general terminological justification for excluding interest-based disobedience from the category of civil disobedience, a justification based on the fact that the term "civil" denotes society's viewpoint as opposed to the sectorial or personal viewpoints existing within society, it is unclear to what extent this exclusion is consistent with the general usage of the term "civil disobedience." This term is apparently also used to denote cases of political disobedience intended to serve interested groups. Moreover, there are also terminological justifications for this usage. For the term "civil" not only denotes the social viewpoint as opposed to the sectorial one. It also denotes the non-military as opposed to the military, or the non-violent as opposed to the violent. Apparently, what many refer to in speaking of "civil disobedience" is a non-military and non-violent political disobedience. A disobedience based on sectorial interests, whose aim is bringing about a change in principles or policies served or expressed by laws, may also be of this type.

[27] As civil disobedience is designed to bring about a change in the policy or the principle served by the law being disobeyed, and as conscientious objection is not intended to achieve these goals, disobedience of the latter type has not been acknowledged as political. This gives expression to an excessively narrow conception of what is political, a conception according to which only acts of disobedience accompanied by full intentions of achieving political results are indeed political. There is no justification either for this conception, or for the conclusion following from it that conscientious objection is not political. It is difficult to see why acts of disobedience which are likely to affect the realization of the principles and goals served or expressed by the laws being disobeyed shouldn't count as political even if they

questions on the justification of civil disobedience and conscientious objection without first replying to the same questions as regards the general type of disobedience discussed in this presentation, a type of which both the above are but sub-classes. I'm referring to disobedience on the basis of objections to the laws being disobeyed. The question if it is justified to disobey a law in order to change it or to protect one's conscience doesn't arise at all if one has no objections to this law. And it is only when such objections justify disobedience that there are grounds to question further whether the act of disobedience should be performed in order to protect one's conscience or in order to bring about a change in the relevant law, or both.

Here I shall address, for the most part, the question whether the goals accompanying disobedience (goals due to which disobedience becomes either civil disobedience or conscientious objection) have any bearing upon the justification of such disobedience *from the point of view of the foundations of the duty to obey.* (As we shall see later, there are additional moral points of view which are relevant to the normative evaluation of these types of disobedience.) Do these goals make any difference, in terms of protecting the institution of law as a tool for enforcing the political morality? Do they make any difference in terms of the equal distribution of the burdens required for the maintenance of this institution, or in terms of the equal distribution of the legal power to exercise political influence?

The answer to the first question is negative as long as the question has to do with the distinction between civil disobedience *simpliciter*, i.e. disobedience intended to bring about changes in the law being disobeyed, and conscientious objection. It is affirmative when the question has to do with the finer .distinction between *coercive civil*

aren't intended to achieve these effects. This is especially true with reference to conscientious objection based on an objection which is conceived of by the objector as applying to humanity in general or at least to his fellow society members. Moreover, disobedience which is based on such an objection is political even if it doesn't, or is unlikely to, have any actual effect on the realization of the goals of the law being disobeyed. It is political as it is, by definition, based on an objection of universal validity, and thus its performer cannot lack an interest in affecting the realization of the goals of the law in question (though he or she may not commit the act of disobedience in order for it to have such an effect). Many acts of conscientious objection, at least the ones placed at the center of public attention in the course of the last two decades – the selective conscientious objection against wars such as that waged by the US in Vietnam, and that waged by Israel in Lebanon – were acts of disobedience based on objections that were, by their very inner logic, of universal or general social validity. Due to this, and due to the results which it was reasonable to expect of them, and which they indeed had, they were political in nature, though they were not necessarily also acts of civil disobedience.

disobedience (which intends to effect a change in, or to frustrate the implementation of, a law or policy), *conscientious objection* and *persuasive civil disobedience*. The distinction between civil disobedience *simpliciter* and conscientious objection is unimportant as it doesn't make much difference in terms of the criteria for justifying disobedience following from the consequence argument. These criteria are related, as we have seen, to the degree to which the reasons on which the objection is based are determined from the point of view of the relevant political morality. It is further related to the force of these reasons, as weighed against the consequences that the disobedience will have regarding the law's functioning in serving this political morality. Both civil disobedience and conscientious objection are disobedience which may be based both on reasons determined by the political morality and on reasons which are not. When they are based on reasons that are not determined by the relevant morality, it is not justified to commit either. When they are based on reasons determined by the morality, their justness depends upon the force of these reasons. This force, in turn, depends upon the nature of the reasons on which the objection is based and upon the specific, concrete conditions under which the question of disobedience is being considered. In terms of the present standard, then, there is no difference between civil disobedience and conscientious objection. In terms of the second standard according to which the justness of disobedience should be decided – that of its anticipated effects on the functioning of the law as a tool for enforcing the political morality – the distinction between civil disobedience *simpliciter* and conscientious objection is too crude. Though the goals of an act of disobedience may affect the seriousness of its consequences regarding the law's authority to determine society's conduct, the levels of this seriousness don't diverge along the border between civil disobedience *simpliciter* and conscientious objection. They diverge along the boundaries between the three-fold distinction cited above, the distinction between coercive civil disobedience, conscientious objection and persuasive civil disobedience. The two types of civil disobedience are situated, in this distinction, on either side of conscientious objection. Coercive civil disobedience poses a graver danger to the law's authority than that posed by conscientious objection. However, persuasive civil disobedience is less dangerous than either of these.[28]

---

[28] In the interval between coercive and persuasive civil disobedience, it is possible to place disobedience to laws intended to caution against the implementation of laws and policies of

This claim is based on the different messages conveyed by each of these types of disobedience as regards the law's authority.

All three types of disobedience may culminate in the frustration of the law's success in realizing its claim to determine society's conduct. All of them imply a readiness to bring this about. However, in the case of disobedience for purposes of persuasion, the threat posed by this willingness is moderated through the opposing message implicit in this type of disobedience. Disobedience for purposes of persuasion also indicates recognition of the law's demand to determine the community's conduct. Just the opposite is true of coercive disobedience. Here, the threat is increased as this type of civil disobedience implies not only a willingness to frustrate the law's success in implementing its demand to determine society's conduct. It also implies a rejection of this demand and even a wish to inherit the law's role in determining conducts. Conscientious objection is situated in between. As it may culminate in the frustration of the law's success in implementing its demand to determine society's conduct, an implied willingness to do this may be attributed to it. The seriousness of this type of disobedience exceeds that of persuasive disobedience, as it doesn't imply a recognition of the law's authority. Its seriousness is less than that of coercive disobedience though. Firstly, it doesn't imply a denial of the law's authority *for all individuals in the society to which the law applies*. It only implies such a denial *for the individuals performing the act of disobedience*. Second, it is less serious as it doesn't indicate the wish of its performers to inherit the law's role as the institution determining society's conducts.

Civil disobedience for purposes of persuasion implies a recognition of the law's demand to determine the conducts of society. The very fact that it is intended to persuade implies this recognition. Though it is, by definition, an illegal manner of persuasion, the change it sets out to achieve in political conditions is not intended to be an illegal one. This form of disobedience is intended to cause the existing legal institutions to change the law, by persuading *them* to do so. Those

types similar to those against which the present protest is aimed. Such an interpretation may be assigned to the objection of Gush Emunim and their followers to evacuate the Raffah Gap, an evacuation which formed one of Israel's commitments under the 1979 peace agreement with Egypt. In refusing to leave their intent was to caution against future peace treaties in which Israel would relinquish the West Bank, less than to undermine the peace treaty with Egypt. Such civil disobedience – "cautionary" civil disobedience – is situated, in terms of the danger it poses to the values protected by the duty to obey the law, between the persuasive and coercive forms of civil disobedience.

who undertake such disobedience must accordingly intend to obey the law at some point in future, even if their attempt to change it should fail. In other words, this type of disobedience leaves the final decision on the nature of society's conduct to the existing legal authorities. The disobedient parties do not intend to supplant the authorities in this capacity. Coercive civil disobedience is situated at the opposite pole. Not only is it *an illegal way to bring about changes* in principles or policies that are served or expressed by various laws. It also expresses *a willingness to accept the fact that the change itself will be illegal*. It expresses a willingness on the part of those who perform it *to supplant the law as the agent determining society's behavior*, at least concerning the matter with regard to which the disobedience is performed. It accordingly indicates a rejection of the law's demand to determine society's conduct, at least on the matter with regard to which the disobedience is performed. Conscientious objection is not, in any way, a means to bring about changes in the law or in its practical success. However, as mentioned earlier, it can in practice lead to such consequences. Like coercive civil disobedience, and unlike persuasive civil disobedience, it does not imply a willingness on the part of its performers to obey the law against which it is committed, at some future point.

It should be noted here that while it is correct that those who commit acts of coercive civil disobedience accordingly express their denial of the law's demand to determine society's conduct, their act doesn't necessarily express their total denial of this demand. Similarly, while it is correct that conscientious objection expresses a willingness to frustrate the actualization of the law's demand to determine the community's conduct, it does not necessarily express a willingness to frustrate this demand altogether. If total denial of the law's demand to determine society's conduct or willingness to frustrate its actualization altogether were logical consequences of conscientious objection and coercive civil disobedience, then these types of disobedience would contradict the very possibility of their performers' acknowledgment of a moral duty to obey the law. This is so, as we have already observed, because the reason justifying the acknowledgment of this duty is partially anchored in the value of the law's existence as an institution determining society's conduct. However, these types of disobedience may agree with an acknowledgment of the moral duty to obey the law, as they do not entail a total denial of the demands of the institution of law to fulfill this role. They may and should express only a partial denial of the law's demand for this role and a willingness to frustrate, only partially, the law's success in fulfilling this role. A person who undertakes to perform such acts of disobedience may express his or her acknowledgment of the law's demand to determine society's conduct in all other areas, by obeying the laws pertaining to these areas even when he or she considers them pertinently defective. He or she may express their acknowledgment of the law's demand to determine conducts, by, among other things, surrendering to its penalties.[29]

The crucial considerations as regards the levels of seriousness of the various types of disobedience under discussion, from the point of view of the argument from consequences, may also aid the substantiation of their levels of seriousness from the point of view of the other foundations for the duty to obey expounded and discussed above. From their point of view too, coercive disobedience is the more serious of the three types. The arguments under which this type of disobedience will be considered the most serious are those presupposing a conception of the law as a tool for determining conducts in society (the general fairness argument, the argument from communal obligations and the argument from the duty of supporting just institutions). This is so for just the reasons due to which it is considered the most serious type of disobedience from the point of view of the argument from consequences. As to the democratic arguments, while persuasive disobedience means a departure from democratic decision procedures in order to accede, in the long run, to their decision, coercive disobedience means the total, albeit perhaps *ad hoc*, denial of the procedure according to which every subject has an equal portion of the legal power of political influence. Conscientious objection too implies a denial of the democratic decision procedure, but it is less serious than coercive disobedience due to its limited goal. It only denies the authority of the decision procedure as regards the conduct of the disobedient party in the relevant matter. It doesn't express a denial of the procedure's authority to determine the conduct of the community as a whole in this matter, or as the agent determining the conduct of the disobedient party in other matters.[30]

---

[29] On submission to punishment see Greenawalt's important comments in *Conflicts of Law and Morality*, pp. 239–40.

[30] One more distinction should be mentioned here – that between direct and indirect civil disobedience. The relation between these two types of disobedience and the persuasive and coercive types of disobedience will help clarify the normative status of these kinds of

What conclusions follow from all of this as regards the performance of acts of disobedience of the three types discussed? As we have seen, in the context of laws which are candidates for disobedience for reasons differing from those of the political morality which the law should serve, the thesis of nearly absolute obedience applies. It seems that such cases of disobedience should be prohibited whether performed as coercive or persuasive civil disobedience. However, the latter would obviously be less serious than the former. As to the breach of such laws in the context of conscientious objection, I have already mentioned a fact to which I will subsequently return in greater detail, i.e. that there are conditions under which the political morality will be able to allow such disobedience.[31]

In cases where it is justified to disobey laws on grounds of objections to their contents, cases where given laws damage the values of the political morality which should be served by the law, the

disobedience. Direct civil disobedience is disobedience in which the law being disobeyed is precisely the law which the act is intended to change (for instance, refusal to enlist in order to prevent a war declared by the state). Indirect civil disobedience is disobedience in which the law whose change is attempted, and the law disobeyed in order to bring about this change, are different ones (for instance, demonstrative road blocks for the prevention of a war which the state intends to enter). It would seem that persuasive civil disobedience would generally, or perhaps always, be indirect, while indirect disobedience would usually be persuasive disobedience. Coercive civil disobedience tends to be direct civil disobedience, at least in part, and direct civil disobedience tends to be coercive. When someone uses disobedience as a means to persuade the government to amend a given law or policy, and disobeys the law in question (or a law serving the policy in question), then clearly the credibility of his or her claim that the disobedience is intended to persuade the government, rather than force it, to amend the law, is seriously damaged. For it is difficult to believe that someone merely wishes to persuade the recognized authorities to amend the law, and not to frustrate its success, when in practice, this person is performing acts which may frustrate the law's success. When I claim that I wish to persuade, but not to force, the government not to go to war, and the laws which I break in order to do so are the mobilization laws, in other words, I refuse to participate in the war, what I'm doing is something that may end in the frustration of the government's policy. How can I claim, at that point, that all I wished was to persuade the government to change its policy, and not to frustrate this policy? The case is entirely different if the laws that I disobey are such that disobedience to them does nothing direct to frustrate the government's policy (for instance, disobeying traffic laws, or laws of symbolic significance such as those prohibiting the physical destruction of I.D. cards, mobilization orders, etc.). The opposite is true of coercive disobedience. If my disobedience is intended to force the government to change its policy or to frustrate the realization of this policy, then the first step that I must take is disobeying the laws that express or serve this policy. I may add indirect disobedience to this direct one. However, it would usually be the case that the main means of frustrating a policy is disobeying the laws that serve it directly. If this is true, then from the viewpoint of the duty to obey the law, direct civil disobedience is the more serious form, while indirect civil disobedience is less serious than conscientious objection. The arguments in the text as to coercive civil disobedience apply to direct civil disobedience as well, and the arguments concerning persuasive civil disobedience conversely apply to the indirect form of civil disobedience.

[31] See pp. 126–7 above, and p. 158 below.

above distinction between the three types of disobedience can facilitate the selection of an act of disobedience which is sensitive to the seriousness of the law's damage to these values. The greater the seriousness of this damage, the stronger the justification to commit an act of disobedience of a more serious nature. The smaller the seriousness of the damage, the stronger the justification to commit a less serious act of disobedience.[32] It is justified to select coercive disobedience when the law blatantly damages important values. It is unjustified to select such disobedience, instead of persuasive or cautionary disobedience,[33] in cases where the damage is obviously less than the above, or when the values being damaged are less important. The distinction between these various forms of disobedience on grounds of objections to the laws' contents carves steps in the slippery slopes created by the complex criterion I proposed earlier for the justification of disobedience. It thus makes the slopes less slippery, to some extent.

So far, I have dealt with the question of the justification of various types of disobedience *from the point of view of the foundations for the duty to obey the law*. As mentioned at the beginning of the present section, this is not the only moral point of view which is relevant to the normative evaluation of the forms of disobedience under discussion. In the case of conscientious objection the above point of view will not supply sufficient grounds for a decision on its justification. Such a decision must also depend on the moral status of conscience. Should every act whose performance is morally justified be conceived of as an act which is justified in terms of conscience? Alternatively, should the group of acts conceived of as justified in terms of conscience be exclusively limited to acts prescribed by important moral principles only, or also, by principles which we conceive of as defining (part of) our identity? If the latter is the correct alternative, then the conclusion is clearly twofold. On the one hand, not every act of disobedience whose performance is morally justified may justifiably be performed in the form of conscientious objection. On the other hand, not every act of disobedience whose performance in the form of conscientious objection is unjustified is a morally unjustified act.

Moreover, the question of the justification of acts of disobedience is the central, but not the only, normative question concerning these acts. Some of these acts raise two other important normative

---

[32] See also Greenawalt, *Conflicts of Law and Morality*, p. 233.   [33] See note 28 above.

questions, in addition to that of their justifiability. First, is there a duty to perform them? Second, how should they be treated once they have been performed? The point of view of the normative considerations that stem from the foundations for the duty to obey will obviously not suffice in order to answer these questions. As regards the second question, I shall show this in detail in the next part of this chapter. As regards the first, it arises chiefly on the subject of civil disobedience. The question whether there is *a duty to perform* acts of this type cannot be answered in the affirmative automatically just because we have given an affirmative answer to the question whether *this performance* is justified. The answer depends on the stance which should be held as regards the individual's responsibility for conduct other than his or her own; his or her responsibility for others' conduct and for the conduct of the society of which he or she is a member.[34] Various theories of political morality may have different positions on this question. Those according to which people are not responsible for acts performed by anyone other than themselves will ordain disobedience to laws when such disobedience is justified, but they will not ordain that such disobedience be intended as a means for the alteration of laws, i.e. as a means for the alteration of society's conduct and the conduct of its members. They will conceive of acts of civil disobedience, when these are justified, as acts which are optional and supererogatory rather than obligatory.[35] Theories of political morality according to which people are responsible not only for the acts that they themselves perform, but also for the morally unjustifiable acts whose performance they do not prevent, will include a duty to perform acts of civil disobedience in cases where they justify this type of disobedience. In the context of this discussion I cannot address the questions bearing upon the position which should be held as to the individual's responsibility for others' conduct.

2. THE ATTITUDE TOWARDS DISOBEDIENCE

A distinction should be drawn, as I have already suggested, between the issue of justifying the appropriate attitude to disobedience and that of justifying the act itself. Such a distinction is mainly warranted

---

[34] On this question see Bernard Williams, "A Critique of Utilitarianism," in J. J. C. Smart and Bernard Williams, *Utilitarianism – For and Against* (Cambridge: Cambridge University Press, 1973).

[35] On actions beyond duty see Heyd, *Supererogation – Its Status in Ethical Theory*.

by the existence of moral and pragmatic considerations that sometimes justify an attitude of tolerance and forgiveness towards disobedience, even when it is unjustified of itself. However, it is also warranted by the existence of considerations that sometimes justify intolerance of disobedience, even when it is justified. My discussion will deal, for the most part, with the first attitude, that of tolerance towards unjustified disobedience. First, though, I shall offer a few brief remarks on the second pole, that of the considerations justifying intolerance of disobedience even when it is justified.

Intolerance of justified acts of disobedience

There are two considerations on which a political morality may ground its authorities' not strictly sympathetic treatment of a disobedience which is, in the morality's own terms, justified from the citizens' point of view. The first of these reasons, both of which are discussed in the first chapter as justifications for the distinction between the rule of law and the duty to obey, is that the argument from consequences is grounded far more powerfully at the junction where the authorities act than it is at the one where the actors are the law's subjects. The second reason has to do with the separation of powers.

As to the first point, the justification of a disobedience based on the law's contents depends, as I have shown, upon the balance between two factors. One scale is occupied by the need to further the political morality's values indirectly, by defending the law's effectiveness as a tool for their enforcement. The opposite scale is occupied by the need for the direct defense of these values. And yet, the considerations involving defense of the law's effectiveness as a means of enforcing a political morality are far more powerful at the junction where the authorities act than they are at the one where the ordinary citizen does. Their weight at the first intersection is much greater as the acts performed here occur well within sight of the public eye and the options for punishing them – unlike those for punishing citizens – are either null or near that. Citizens' disobedience would only cause significant doubt that the law was in good working order, were the authorities to refrain from enforcing it. A failure on the part of the authorities to apply the law would leave no alternative other than such doubts. The acts in question are such that their identity as breaches of law is undisputable. Thus, any failure on the part of the prosecuting authorities to bring their authors to trial or, on the part of the judicial authorities, to convict and punish these authors, must raise doubts as to whether the law is possessed of a mouthpiece and an executor, or doubts about its very existence. Moreover, failure to bring to trial and/or to convict, as well as failure to punish are (or can at least be taken to be) expressions of resignation towards, and even encouragement of, disobedience.

The law enforcement authorities can furthermore not indulge in such failures for reasons of the separation of powers. Recurrent conduct of this type would blur the boundaries between these and the legislative and policy-making authorities. (The last, on the other hand, may become convinced that the opposition to the law or policies, upon which the disobedience was based, is indeed just. In such cases they will amend these laws or policies and should also utilize their authority of mitigation, thus showing their gratitude and sympathy towards the agents that brought the mistake to their attention.)

The attitude towards justified disobedience depends on the balance between considerations of precisely the same nature as those that determine the justifiability of the disobedience itself. Conversely, the attitude towards unjustified disobedience depends on an entirely different balance. Here one of the scales alone is occupied both by the need for direct furtherance of the values that the law is designed to serve and the need for indirect furtherance of these values through protection of the law's effectivity as a tool for their enforcement. In this case the two together support a hostile reaction to the act of disobedience. Though it may, at times, be right to abstain from such a reaction, this is not because these considerations somehow suddenly cease to exist. If it is sometimes right to react differently, this is only because other, different considerations occupy the opposite scale. The considerations on this side support tolerance towards unjustified disobedience. What, exactly, are these considerations and how does one determine when they override the considerations in favor of the "natural," hostile reaction towards unjustified disobedience?

Three types of considerations are possible candidates for the role of supporting tolerance: considerations of fairness, considerations of moral pragmatics, considerations stemming from values such as freedom of conscience and personal autonomy. Most of my efforts as regards considerations of fairness will be spent on their rejection as acceptable foundations for tolerance. In discussing the pragmatic considerations, I will try, for the most part, to clarify their contingent character as foundations for tolerance. The remaining considerations, then, are those of the freedom of conscience and personal autonomy. The major thrust of their treatment here will address the questions when and how they should be expressed.

Tolerance of unjustified disobedience: considerations of fairness

According to the thesis of limited obedience discussed above, theories of political morality will often justify disobedience of laws which are harmful to their values. In the context of contradictory political theories, the practical conclusions following from this thesis will often be contradictory. When a given law or policy causes significant harm to the values of a specific political morality, in accordance with that morality, this law should be disobeyed. If another political morality contradicts the first as regards the values in question, it follows by this assumption that its practical instructions will contradict those of the first morality, and vice versa. In societies whose members subscribe to opposing theories of political morality, it would seem unfair of their members to view disobedience based on their own values as justified while denying the right of their political opponents to a disobedience based on their values. Though they deny the justness of a disobedience based on the values of the opponent morality, they should, it seems, acknowledge the opponent subscribers' right to disobey.

Is one really being unfair when allowing oneself to disobey the law because it harms the values of one's political morality, while disallowing others' disobedience for the values of theirs? An argument offered by Raz, in a similar context, supplies grounds for a negative answer to this question.

[A] person who supports his action [of disobedience] by argument to show that it is in defense of a just cause can without unfairness deny a right to civil disobedience. He allows others to perform similar actions in pursuit of similarly just aims. He denies both himself and others the right to disobey in support of morally wrong aims.[36]

In other words, when a person breaks the law for the sake of moral values, the justification for this disobedience lies in the values

---

[36] See Raz, *The Authority of Law*, p. 270.

themselves and not in the fact of his or her subscription to them. What fairness requires of a person, then, is to allow others' disobedience on the basis of these values. It doesn't require the person to allow others' disobedience on the basis of the values to which they subscribe. Disobedience for moral reasons is just the same as any other act performed for such reasons. People who act on the basis of such reasons do not act on the basis of the fact that they believe in such reasons. This fact may be the *cause* of their actions. It is not the *justification* for their actions. The justification lies in the reasons themselves, not in the fact of believing in them. The justification for my telling the truth is *that people should tell the truth* and not *that I believe* that people should tell the truth. Thus, if you believe that people should lie, it would be foolish to require me to allow you to lie, in the interests of fairness. What fairness requires is that I allow you what I allow myself, namely, to act on the basis of the principle that people should tell the truth.

According to the present argument, similar things must be said of disobedience which is based on moral justifications. If a Gush-Emunim member disobeys the law forbidding him or her to settle in Judea, the justification for its breach lies in the principle of fatherland's integrity, not in the fact that he or she believes in this principle. Fairness requires a person to allow others to do the same, namely, to disobey laws which contradict this principle. It doesn't require that he or she allow others to disobey laws that contradict any principles to which they may subscribe. It doesn't, for instance, require that he or she allow the members of Yesh Gvul (a movement of conscientious objectors to army service in the occupied territories) to disobey the laws compelling them to oppress the Arabs of the West Bank, as they believe in a principle prohibiting the subjection and oppression of another nation. By the same token, the latter, in breaking the laws compelling them to oppress the Arabs of the West Bank, do so on the basis of the principle prohibiting the oppression of people's legitimate aspirations, and not on the basis of the fact that they believe in this principle. Fairness thus requires them to allow others' disobedience of laws that serve policies of oppression. It doesn't require them to allow the members of Gush Emunim to disobey the laws prohibiting the settlement of Judea, as they in turn believe in the principle of the fatherland's integrity. Fairness doesn't oblige someone who believes in the principle of telling the truth to tolerate liars. Similarly, it doesn't oblige someone who believes in a principle supporting the violation of orders to guard a settlement to tolerate violations of the laws that prohibit settling. Fairness does not require a believer that lying is permissible to allow a believer in telling the truth to tell it. Similarly, it doesn't oblige the subscribers to principles entailing violation of the laws prohibiting settlement to allow others to disobey orders to guard the settlements. Fairness is irrelevant to the justness of telling the truth or lying. Deciding which of the two acts is right depends on the decision which of the two principles is right – that of telling the truth or that of lying. In exactly the same manner the issue of which laws may legitimately be disobeyed – those ordaining that the settlement be guarded or those prohibiting settlement – is one that has nothing to do with fairness. Its answer, rather, depends upon the question which of the two is the valid principle – the one forbidding one people to rule another or the one ordaining the fatherland's integrity.

This rejection of the attempt to base tolerance of unjustified disobedience on fairness, elicited from Raz's argument against the right to civil disobedience, is fundamentally sound. However, before its final placement within the present context, one serious reservation should be aired and answered. Raz, in offering this argument, overlooks one of the rationales for the existence of the institutions of government and law, i.e. the need for institutions that supply practical solutions to questions arousing public controversy. When you acknowledge the moral duty to obey the law for this reason, but work against the solutions it supplies for the very reasons behind your original stance in the controversy, you would, it seems, be contradicting yourself. It would seem that you believe it right to abstain from action based on these considerations, despite their correctness, while you conversely believe it right not to forgo actions based on these considerations. A decision has to be made. Adherence to a firm belief in the duty to obey the law, on the present grounds, obliges one to refrain from relying on the correctness of one's stance in the controversy, as a rationale for action against the solution assigned this controversy by the law. If you nevertheless act on the basis of this stance, you do so, so it seems, not because it is right but because it is yours. And if you allow yourself action on the basis of your position because it is yours, you are required by fairness to allow others the same thing, namely to act on the basis of views because they are theirs.

It is worthwhile emphasizing that the claim being made here is not one of moral skepticism. It doesn't stem from the position that there is no right or wrong in matters of morality. Even if this skeptical stance were correct, the present discussion would be barred from assuming it. Its very existence presupposes the possibility of rationally persuading readers or listeners of the existence of justified and unjustified cases of disobedience. Were this an impossibility, then all cases of disobedience would, it seems, be morally permissible as nothing would be morally forbidden. The present discussion would then turn out to be a waste of time and ink, as its central question was which cases of disobedience are justified and which cases should be treated tolerantly. My claim that the opposing sides of a public controversy cannot rely upon the correctness of their positions is, then, not based on a rejection of the possibility that one of these sides is indeed correct. It is based on the fact that these opponents, inasmuch as they have acknowledged their duty to obey the law due to the need for an institution supplying practical solutions to controversial problems, have made a commitment to abstain from reliance on the correctness of their positions on the controversy. A failure on their parts to keep this commitment obliges them, for reasons of fairness, to permit their opponents to do the same.

This argument can be used not only in attempts to contend for tolerance of illegitimate violations. It may also be used in attempts to deny the possibility that violations based on objections to the substance of laws could ever be justified. In fact, however, it won't serve either of these purposes. Its pertinence is limited to the sphere where the law serves to supply controversies with practical solutions.[37] Deep-rooted conflicts between theories of political morality cannot fall within this sphere. As we have already seen, any attempt to offer moral grounds for the duty to obey the law necessarily assumes the existence of a political morality the principles of which supply the basis for this duty. I have tried to claim that any political morality, whatever its principles, will need a legal system to implement its values and decide the outcome of controversies in its areas of indeterminacy. It is unjustified to act against its decisions on such matters. No political morality, however, will need the law to decide issues on subjects on which it is definitive. As I have already clarified, were a political morality to leave the decision of such issues to the law, the result might be self-contradiction. Thus, when the law decides on issues where deeprooted conflicts exist between opposing

---

[37] On this matter see also the last part of chapter 1, above.

political theories, the claim that a subscriber to the duty to obey must forgo reliance on his or her position in the conflict simply doesn't apply. Disobedience of the law that is based on positions of this type obliges the violators, for reasons of fairness, to allow others' disobedience on the basis of the same positions. Fairness doesn't oblige them to be tolerant of unjustified disobedience.

Some will undoubtedly claim that specific situations justify the law's conception not only as an institution for the decision of controversies within a single political morality, but as one which should decide between rival political moralities such as nationalism or fascism and liberalism. They may claim that in such cases people should consequently not disobey laws in the interests of the values of their political morality. Thus, nationalists shouldn't disobey the law even when the policy it serves does disservice to the nation. Liberals shouldn't disobey it even when it harms liberties such as the freedom of speech or assembly. If nationalists nonetheless disobey laws that damage their values, the principle of fairness requires them to permit liberals' disobedience of laws that damage theirs and vice versa.

Let's assume these claims are correct. Let's assume, in other words, the existence of specific situations in which the law should justly be conceived of as an institution which decides between opposing theories such as nationalism or fascism and liberalism. What, then, is the status of the justifications for this conception of the law, and what are its implications for the topic under discussion? There are two answers to this question. First, these may be pragmatic justifications. In such cases, prohibiting disobedience to the law and fairness-based tolerance would both be of a strictly contingent and instrumental value. Second, such justifications may be considered to be moral. In such cases it may turn out that what they mean, in practice, is a sacrifice of at least the actual implementation of the values informing one or both of the rival political moralities.

As regards the second possibility, when a moral nature is ascribed to the justification for viewing the law as an institution which decides between rival theories, this follows either from a third political morality, thought to transcend the first two, or from a combination of the two which yields yet a third morality. In these cases, the areas where the two moralities clash are, in fact, the areas of the third's indeterminacy. Violations of the laws deciding issues that lie within these areas are thus unjustified. People who violate them anyway, on the basis of their positions, are obliged by the principle of fairness to allow others the same privilege. Though this is an outline of the strictly formal aspects of such a situation, the implications of these formalities may, as happens in many other cases, afford substantive applications. People may believe, then, that there are moral justifications for viewing a given legal system as an institution deciding between nationalism and liberalism. According to the formal explication above, they must consequently understand that they are actually subscribing to a third political morality. They must furthermore understand that their adoption of this morality necessarily involves a willingness to relinquish, at least in practice, the values of the morality to which they formerly subscribed. This is so as a political morality that gives the law the power of decision between nationalism and liberalism is almost completely devoid of values, either of those of nationalism or those of liberalism. It is empty, as most of the fundamental values of the two theories are diametrically opposed to each other, and a political morality comprising both will be composed, almost completely, of principles and their contradictions. It will thus be almost totally indeterminate. In point of fact, it won't supply practical guidance on almost any matter. In other words, people who believe that there are moral justifications for viewing the law as the arbitrator between the theory of political values in which they believe and another, diametrically opposed theory, are in fact willing to continue subscribing to their professed values theoretically at the very most. They are willing not to subscribe to them in practice. As stated though, the law can be conceived of as an institution deciding between rival political theories for pragmatic rather than moral reasons.

Tolerance of unjustified disobedience: pragmatic considerations

People who subscribe to a political morality and share a political–legal system with subscribers to a rival political morality may gather that violation of the law in the interests of their values will cause their opponents to do the same, i.e. violate the law in the interests of their own values. This may seriously weaken the political–legal system. Consequently, damage may be done not only to the implementation of the rival values, but to that of their own. If the implementation of their values is to suffer more damage in this manner than would be the case were the law to be obeyed, then *the pragmatics of their values' implementation* supplies reasons for obeying the law, in the absence of which its violation would be justified. These are also reasons for tolerating unjustified disobedience of laws that would not be justly tolerated in the absence of these pragmatic considerations.

Pragmatic considerations can often receive moral support. One must keep in mind, however, that despite the presence of such support, their validity depends upon the specific occasion created by the practical state of affairs. This occasion can prescribe either the law's violation or its non-violation with the same degree of cogency. Similarly, it can generate equally valid instructions either for intolerance of unjustified violations or for tolerance of such violations. When rival political moralities are possessed of equal social power, they will prescribe equal obedience to the laws opposing their values and equal disobedience to those that further them. Clearly, however, this is a pseudo-moral fairness. Neither of the rival theories recognize the current need for equality and tolerance out of respect for the fact that people may believe in values contradicting its own. It does so in the interests of the best implementation of its values that is possible under the present conditions. In other words, in this case, fairness and tolerance are imperatives, not because of any inherent value they may possess. They draw their validity from contingent pragmatic considerations. Any shift in the balance of social power between the rival moralities will entail what, from the standpoint of the stronger theory, are moral justifications for increasing its disobedience of the laws that damage its values and decreasing its tolerance towards violations of the laws that further them.

Tolerance of unjustified disobedience: freedom of conscience

A third consideration possibly making it justified to show tolerance towards unjustified breaches of the law is that of the principle of freedom of conscience. Such tolerance is not only a means to other ends. It is of intrinsic value. In accordance with the principle in question, people should be allowed to conduct their lives according to the dictates of their consciences. The foundations and validity of this principle lie outside the scope of this discussion, yet several points concerning it are worthwhile keeping in mind. First of all, the principle of freedom of conscience only has actual practical import within the framework of a humanist–liberal political morality. Freedom of conscience will only be taken seriously by political moralities that focus on individual well-being (and are accordingly humanistic) and view the individual's freedom in choosing values and commitments, and his or her success in living by these values and commitments, as central to his or her well-being (and are accordingly liberal). Second, freedom of conscience means the freedom to act on the dictates of conscience for the sole reason that they are given by the conscience, regardless of their justness or of the correctness of their contents. Freedom of conscience means the freedom to act on the dictates of conscience even though they may be wrong.[38] Were the validity of this freedom dependent on the dictates' rightness, it would be devoid of practical content. It is equivalent, in this sense, to the value of freedom of speech. This value too, were it subordinated to the justifiability or correctness of the enunciations allowed under it, would be devoid of practical significance.

What this means in the context of the duty to obey the law is that freedom of conscience is a possible basis for tolerance of unjust violations of this duty. It doesn't mean that the principle necessarily tips the scales in favor of such tolerance. In order to do so it must compete successfully with the justifications in favor of the duty to obey and, usually and more significantly, with the justifications for the specific law being disobeyed. An unjust violation of the duty to obey may be so because it is based on unjustified objections to the violated law (e.g. when someone objects to just income tax laws which don't warrant such objection and should accordingly not be violated). On the other hand, it may be unjustified because it is based on just objections to the violated law which are nonetheless not reason enough for its violation (e.g. when someone violates unjust tax laws that are such that their unjustness isn't sufficient to justify their violation). In cases of the second type, freedom of conscience must only compete against the need to protect the law as the means enforcing the political morality. In cases of the first type, it will be competing against this need and against the risk that the violation in question will endanger the specific ends whose implementation the specific law attempted (i.e. in the example above, the just re-distribution of income).

The situation here is no different from that of any other conflict of values. It involves, on the one hand, the need to respect freedom of conscience, one of the values of a liberal political morality. On the other hand it involves the need to support one of the other values furthered (so we've assumed) by the violated law, and the need to protect the legal system as the means for enforcing the values of this

---

[38] See also Raz, *The Authority of Law*, p. 277, and D. Richards, "Conscience, Human Rights, and the Anarchist Challenge to the Obligation to Obey the Law," *Georgia Law Review* 18 (1984), 771, note 17.

morality. Permitting disobedience on the basis of unjust objections to the law's contents means permitting the disobedient agents to obstruct, endanger and neutralize the values for whose realization the law was enacted (as our subject is disobedience on the basis of *unjust* objections to the laws' contents). On the other hand, prohibiting such disobedience means prohibiting the realization of the principle of freedom of conscience which is also one of the values of a liberal political morality and should thus be furthered by the law.

This dilemma should be solved in the usual manner used to solve moral dilemmas (when a solution is at all possible) – by balancing the conflicting values against each other. Freedom of conscience should be balanced against the values protected by the law whose violation is being considered, qualified by the amount of damage to be sustained by these values due to the violation, as well as the likelihood that such damage will actually occur. When the issue involves disobedience to a law furthering a value which is inferior to freedom of conscience, the solution should be official, selective exemption from the law. For instance, when a law obliges someone to wear a uniform prohibited by their religion, this person should be officially exempted from wearing uniform. When someone disobeys a law that implements a value more important than freedom of conscience, and permitting this law's violation means significant danger or damage to its implementation, disobedience should be prohibited. For instance, take a settler who refuses, for reasons of conscience, to evacuate the land of the Raffah Gap, after Israel has agreed to its evacuation in the peace treaty with Egypt. Clearly, the state cannot allow such a violation. Were it to do so this would mean Israel's failure to fulfill the terms of the peace treaty. This would involve damage to two values which, at least when taken together, seem more important than freedom of conscience: those of furthering peace and respecting significant international agreements. When the violation doesn't frustrate the value's realization but only endangers it slightly, the case against tolerance of such a violation is far weaker than the previous one. Take, for example, a soldier who holds the political views of Gush Emunim, and refuses to obey the orders given his unit to forcefully evict the settlers of the Raffah Gap after the peace treaty. In this case, unlike that of the settlers who refuse to leave their land, there is room for tolerance. Permitting the soldier's non-participation in the settlers' forceful eviction will not mean failure to fulfill the terms of the peace treaty. The objecting soldier can be replaced with another one who will carry out the task of eviction.

According to the present argument, then, a liberal political morality may show tolerance towards disobedience which is based upon values opposing its own. If it is, indeed, capable of tolerating such disobedience it can certainly, under similar conditions, tolerate disobedience based on practical considerations towards which it is neutral, aesthetic considerations for example or considerations of economic efficacy. Manifestations of tolerance of this type may be of importance to various professionals. Some of these have strong views on the subjects of their expertise. They tend to develop what is commonly referred to as a "professional conscience." Such people may, at times, object strongly to various laws relating to the areas of their expertise. When the practical consequences of these laws' violations don't frustrate or significantly endanger their ends, such violations can be permitted. The nearly absolute obedience thesis presented in the first section of this discussion considers such violations unjustified. As it emerges here, their unjustness doesn't necessarily make them impermissible.[39]

The previous section of this chapter discussed distinctions between various types of disobedience, based on objections to the contents of the violated laws. It dealt, especially, with the distinction between civil disobedience for purposes of coercion, civil disobedience for purposes of persuasion and conscientious objection. Needless to say, the claim for tolerance examined here (unlike the claims for tolerance on the basis of fairness or pragmatic considerations) supports only tolerance of what is construed as conscientious objection.[40] Nothing said here supports tolerance towards either type of civil disobedience. Nothing said here indicates that political moralities have any reason to tolerate civil disobedience aimed at changing the law or the government's policy in the interests of values that are foreign to them. I have described civil disobedience for purposes of coercion that is

[39] This point clarifies the second qualification outlined above to the thesis of nearly absolute obedience. See pp. 126–7 above.

[40] I am purposely speaking of actions perceived as conscientious objection, and not of actions intended as such by their authors, as many of those who disobey laws on the basis of objections to their contents intend their disobedience as both civil disobedience and conscientious objection. In order to decide whether to tolerate these acts of disobedience, even if they were only intended as conscientious objection, we must, as explained in the text, check the degree of danger they pose to the values that should be furthered, as well as the importance of these values relative to the value of freedom of conscience. If the fact that someone who disobeys intends his or her act as civil disobedience as well does nothing to increase the actual danger to the values that should be furthered, it would seem that this act of disobedience should continue to be viewed as conscientious objection, although it is also an act of civil disobedience.

based on values of this kind, as the severer type of violation. Prohibition of this type of civil disobedience will thus be especially stringent. Civil disobedience for purposes of persuasion which is based on values of this kind was described above as the less severe of the two. Though the present thesis prohibits it as well, the injunction will be less stringent in this case.

Various means for expressing tolerance

Tolerance of unjust disobedience to the law may be expressed in several ways. It is advisable to answer the question whether or not the reasons in favor of tolerance override those against it in combination with an answer to the question, how is this tolerance to be expressed? Tolerance may be expressed in the law itself or through granting exemptions from the law, so that whoever acts on grounds of conscientious objection will automatically be exempted from the legal duty to which he or she conscientiously objects. It may be expressed in the form of criminal defense, so that whoever acts on the basis of her or his conscientious objection will be committing a breach of legal duty but will nonetheless be exempt from criminal responsibility for this breach. Tolerance may furthermore be expressed through the law's application rather than its wording. The authorities implementing the law, those determining the form of its actual implementation and those enforcing it through charges, trials and sentences, may employ the discretion at their disposal for the realization of their authority. They may take disobedience into consideration when determining the ways of actually enforcing the law or when deciding the severity of the possible sentences. Expressing tolerance through the law itself, either in the form of exemptions from the legal duty arousing the disobedience or in the form of exemptions from criminal responsibility for this duty's breach, is considerably advantageous to the other ways of expressing tolerance, from the standpoint of various aspects of the principle of rule of law. Such tolerance is far more likely to apply equally to all of the law's subjects than a tolerance whose expression is left to the authorities' discretion. It is also more likely to be promulgated than the second form of tolerance.[41] And yet, in some cases it would seem better that tolerance be expressed by those in charge of determining just how the law is to be used for the actual implementation of the policies

[41] See also Greenawalt, *Conflicts of Law and Morality*, p. 276.

arousing disobedience, and by those in charge of charging, judging and punishing violators of the law. The cases I have in mind are those in which disobedience is especially problematic: objection to a specific war or a specific peace treaty, for instance. It would seem, in such cases, that the authorities implementing the policy and accordingly employing various laws, especially mobilization laws, should begin by showing as much consideration as possible towards conscientious objectors as they allocate soldiers for the various missions necessary. In other words, they should try, as far as is possible, to assign the objectors to duties which don't go against their consciences. When they have exhausted their ability to show such consideration, conscientious objectors should be tried, and the severity of their punishment dictated by the size of the risks their objection creates for the implementation of the policies it endangers. The lower the numbers of such objectors, the lower the risk their objection creates for the policies against which it is directed. The courts will accordingly be able to express a higher degree of respect and tolerance towards the objectors' consciences, through sentences that are comparatively light. The higher the objectors' numbers, the greater the risk their objection poses for the implementation of the policies against which it is directed. This decreases the leeway for an active expression of tolerance towards their violations, in the form of comparatively light sentences. This mode of reaction to unjust violations is successful as it is sensitive to the specific conditions relevant to the balance according to which unjust violations should be treated, i.e. the balance between the need to implement the policy against which the objection is directed and the need to show respect for the objectors' consciences.

This type of reaction may have the semblance of injustice. A mounting number of conscientious objectors increasingly endangers the policies against which the objection is directed. As a result, there will be a decrease in the degree of tolerance that the courts are free to show towards the objectors, in the form of light sentences. This will mean unequal sentences for seemingly identical violations. In fact, though, no injustice is done here, as the violations only seem identical. They are not truly so. The answer to the question, what is the danger involved for the policies against which the objection is directed, is one that changes as the numbers change. This danger is an important component of the description of these violations, necessary for an assessment of the moral reaction appropriate to them. The greater the numbers of the objectors to a war or a peace treaty, the greater the danger to the policy of war or peace. If someone objects when there are many such objectors and consequently receives less tolerant treatment than that shown previously, when the objectors were few, he or she cannot complain of any injustice. The fact of his or her objection when many others are objecting should be taken into account in an assessment of the objection's moral severity. Such an objector is consequently not entitled to the same treatment received by others who acted while the number of objectors was small.

Afterword

I have tried, in this book, to defend the duty to obey the law on two fronts. I have tried to defend it against the attack on its very existence attempted by many philosophers, and against the corruptive use made of it by politicians and public figures.

Of the philosophers who would deny the existence of the duty to obey the law, some claim that the attempts to ground it have failed. I have demonstrated, in the second and third chapters, that there are some attempts that succeed. Their success, however, is not complete. They support a duty to perform actions because these have been ordered by law. This duty, if it applies at all, applies to everyone. But it doesn't apply in every case. It doesn't apply to unjust political systems, and, in the context of just systems, it doesn't apply to all laws in all the occasions to which they apply. Disobedience which will cause no damage whatsoever, either to the goal served by the given law, or to the operation of the institution of law as a tool for instituting and enforcing desirable conducts, is disobedience which cannot be questioned on the basis of any of the grounds of the duty to obey.

Other philosophers who would deny the existence of the duty to obey try to do so on the basis of the alleged contradiction between this duty and moral autonomy. They believe that various aspects of the meaning of the duty to obey entail the conclusion that its acknowledgment means the individual's surrender of independent judgment and/or subsequent action. I have shown, in the first chapter, that this view is incorrect. Acknowledgment of the duty to obey the law does not entail a surrender of independent judgment and/or subsequent action. Like any other moral duty, it entails a surrender of the possibility of its breach on the basis of specific types of reasons only, not on the basis of all possible types of reasons.

The last chapter introduced the reasons dominated by the duty to obey, the reasons which we have relinquished as grounds for action in cases where the duty to obey applies. It also introduced the reasons which are not dominated by the duty to obey, the reasons with which it is forced to compete. The first are amoral reasons, reasons of self-interest, of economic effectivity, aesthetic reasons, and so forth. The others are moral reasons. These are not overridden by the duty to obey without careful consideration. It must be weighed against them in the light of criteria which I have outlined. These last points form my attempt to defend the duty to obey from the corruptive use made of it by politicians and public figures.

I have not given an exhaustive answer to the question of the limits of obedience. What I have said on the subject that is valid for any theory of political morality – the thesis that follows from the argument from consequences – is, as stated, totally formal. Moreover, most of my more substantive claims – those arising from the foundations of the duty to obey anchored in democracy and fairness, and those touching upon tolerance towards disobedience – depend upon the validity of a humanistic political morality. Nothing has been said here of this validity. The limits I have outlined for the duty to obey the law are thus either formal and devoid of substance, or less formal but dependent upon the validity of humanism.

The formality of the core of my answer as to the limits of the duty to obey is of certain value. It is of value as it can aid anyone who has decided upon the values to which he or she adheres, whatever their nature, in determining these limits. It is suited to any set of values. Yet it is chiefly of value as it does *only* this. In this manner it stresses the fact that the duty to obey the law is not possessed of moral omnipotence. It stresses the limitations of this duty's strength. It underlines the responsibility of each individual in making more basic value decisions, as a condition for reaching a moral decision on the limits of the duty to obey. This duty, despite the fact of its importance, is necessarily a secondary one. It is intended to serve other values and duties upon which it is dependent.

The partial and conditional nature of my answer to the question of the limits of the duty to obey is of value not only because it stresses the limitations of the *moral strength* of this duty. It is also of value as it stresses the limitations of its *social strength* in societies suffering from a lack of consensus on values. In many societies, at least during given periods in their histories, there is more than one prevalent political morality. At times the values of one of these moralities are in direct opposition to those of another. In such societies there is often an expectation that the moral duty to obey the law will bridge the gaps between values and form the moral cement that unifies the society. Experience shows that this is frequently a vain expectation. This was the case in the United States prior to the abolition of slavery. This was the case in the German Weimar Republic. It was the case in Russia before the October revolution. What occurs in such societies is the disappearance of one of the sets of rival values; through the disappearance of those who adhere to these values, through their concealment of the fact that they hold these values, through their abandonment of these values, or through a combination (to varying degrees) of all three. This is all familiar to most of us. I have tried to show, here, that it is logically inevitable. It follows, necessarily, from the dependence of the law, the duty to obey it and the limits of this duty, on the substantive values of a political morality.

Bibliography
(including only works cited or referred to)

In this bibliography all cross-references to edited collections of articles, etc. are by author or editor and short title. Each such collection is listed in its own right under the editor's or author's name, with full bibliographical details.

Aiken, Henry D. (ed.), *Hume's Moral and Political Philosophy*, New York: Hafner Press, 1948

Aquinas, St. Thomas, *Summa Theologica*, London: Blackfriars, 1966

Arenson, R., "The Principle of Fairness and Free-Rider Problems," *Ethics* 92 (1982), 616

Beran, Harry, "In Defense of the Consent Theory of Political Obligation and Authority," *Ethics* 87 (1976–7), 260

"What is the Basis of Political Authority?" *Monist* 66 (1983), 487

Boardman, W. S., "Coordination and the Moral Obligation to Obey the Law," *Ethics* 97 (1987), 546

Carr, C. L., "The Problem of Political Authority," *Monist* 66 (1983), 472

Daniels, Norman (ed.), *Reading Rawls*, New York: Basic Books, 1975

Dworkin, Ronald, "The Original Position" in Daniels (ed.), *Reading Rawls*, 16

A Matter of Principle, Cambridge, Mass.: Harvard University Press, 1985

Law's Empire, Cambridge, Mass.: Harvard University Press, 1986

Finnis, John, "The Authority of Law in the Predicament of Contemporary Social Theory," *Notre Dame Journal of Law, Ethics and Public Policy* 1 (1984), 115

Flathman, R. E., *The Practice of Political Authority*, Chicago: Chicago University Press, 1980

Fuller, Lon L., *The Morality of Law* (revised edition), New Haven: Yale University Press, 1969

Gans, Chaim, "Mandatory Rules and Exclusionary Reasons," *Philosophia* 15 (1985–6), 373

"The Obligation to Obey the Law, Comment" in Gavison (ed.), *Issues in Contemporary Legal Philosophy – The Influence of H. L. A. Hart*, 180

"The Normativity of Law and its Co-ordinative Function," *Israel Law Review* 16 (1981), 333

Gavison, Ruth (ed.), *Issues in Contemporary Legal Philosophy – The Influence of H. L. A. Hart*, Oxford: Oxford University Press, 1987

Glover, Jonathan, *Causing Death and Saving Lives*, Harmondsworth: Penguin, 1977

Godwin, William, *Enquiry Concerning Political Justice*, ed. I. Kramnick, Harmondsworth: Penguin, 1976

Green, T. H., *Lectures on the Principles of Political Obligation*, London: Longmans, 1907

Greenawalt, Kent, *Conflicts of Law and Morality*, Oxford: Oxford University Press, 1987

Harman, Gilbert, "Reasons" in Raz (ed.), *Practical Reasoning*

Hart, H. L. A., "Are There Any Natural Rights?" *Philosophical Review* 64 (1955), 175

   The Concept of Law, Oxford: Oxford University Press, 1961

   Essays on Bentham, Oxford: Oxford University Press, 1982

Heyd, David, *Supererogation – Its Status in Ethical Theory*, Cambridge: Cambridge University Press, 1982

Hobbes, Thomas, *Leviathan*, Indianapolis: Bobbs-Merrill, 1958

Honore, A. M., "Must We Obey? Necessity as a Ground of Obligation," *Virginia Law Review* 67 (1981) 39

Hook, Sidney (ed.), *Law and Philosophy*, New York: New York University Press, 1964

Hooker, Richard, *Of the Laws of Ecclesiastical Polity*, Cambridge: Cambridge University Press, 1989

Hume, David, "Of the Original Contract" in Aiken (ed.), *Hume's Moral and Political Philosophy*, 356

Kelsen, Hans, *General Theory of Law and State*, New York: Russel and Russel, 1961

Klosko, G., "The Principle of Fairness and Political Obligation," *Ethics* 97 (1986–7), 353

Kronman, A., "Contract Law and Distributive Justice," *Yale Law Journal* 89 (1980), 472

Locke, John, *Two Treatises of Government*, Cambridge: Cambridge University Press, 1960

Lyons, David, *Forms and Limits of Utilitarianism*, Oxford: Oxford University Press, 1965

Machan, T., "Individualism and the Problem of Political Authority," *Monist* 66 (1983), 500

McCloskey, H. J., *Meta-Ethics and Normative Ethics*, The Hague: Martinus Nijhoff, 1969

Mill, J. S., *Representative Government*, London: Dent, 1960

Miller, David, *Anarchism*, London: Dent and Sons, 1984

Moore, Michael, "Authority, Law and Razian Reasons," *Southern California Law Review* 62 (1989), 827

Nozick, Robert, *Anarchy, State and Utopia*, Oxford: Basil Blackwell, 1974

Olsen, F., "Socrates on Legal Obligation: Legitimation Theory and Civil Disobedience," *Georgia Law Review* 18 (1984), 929

Plamenatz, John, *Man and Society*, London: Longman, 1963
  Consent, Freedom and Political Obligation, 2nd edition, Oxford: Oxford University Press, 1968
Plato, *Crito*, in B. Jowett (trans.), *The Dialogues of Plato*, New York: Pocket Books, inc., 1950
Rawls, John, "Legal Obligation and the Duty of Fair Play" in Hook (ed.), *Law and Philosophy*
  A Theory of Justice, Cambridge, Mass.: Harvard University Press, 1971
Raz, Joseph, *The Concept of a Legal System*, Oxford: Oxford University Press, 1970
  Practical Reason and Norms, London: Hutchinson, 1975
  (ed.) *Practical Reasoning*, Oxford: Oxford University Press, 1978
  The Authority of Law, Oxford: Oxford University Press, 1979
  "Authority and Consent," *Virginia Law Review* (1981), 103
  "The Obligation to Obey: Revision and Tradition," *Notre Dame Journal of Law, Ethics and Public Policy* 1 (1984), 139
  The Morality of Freedom, Oxford: Oxford University Press, 1986
Reiman, J. H., *In Defense of Political Philosophy*, New York: Harper, 1972
Richards, David, *A Theory of Reasons For Action*, Oxford: Oxford University Press, 1971
  "Conscience, Human Rights, and the Anarchist Challenge to the Obligation to Obey the Law," *Georgia Law Review* 18 (1984), 771
Ross, W. D., *The Right and the Good*, Oxford: Oxford University Press, 1930
Rousseau, Jean Jacques, *The Social Contract*, London: Everyman, 1950
Sartorius, Rolf, "Hart's Concept of Law" in Summers (ed.), *More Essays in Legal Philosophy*
  "Political Authority and Political Obligation," *Virginia Law Review* 67 (1981), 3
Searle, J. R., "*Prima Facie* Obligations" in Raz (ed.), *Practical Reasoning*
Simmons, A. J., *Moral Principles and Political Obligations*, Princeton: Princeton University Press, 1979
  "Voluntarism and Political Associations," *Virginia Law Review* 67 (1981), 19
  "Consent, Free Choice and Democratic Government," *Georgia Law Review* 18 (1984), 791
Singer, Peter, *Democracy and Disobedience*, Oxford: Oxford University Press, 1973
  Practical Ethics, Cambridge: Cambridge University Press, 1979
Smart, J. J. C., and Williams, B., *Utilitarianism – For and Against*, Cambridge: Cambridge University Press, 1973
Smith, M. B. E., "Is There a *Prima Facie* Obligation to Obey the Law?" *Yale Law Journal* 82 (1973), 950
Soper, Philip, "The Obligation to Obey the Law" in Gavison (ed.), *Issues in Contemporary Legal Philosophy – The Influence of H. L. A. Hart*, 127
Strawson, P. F., "Ethical Intuitionism," *Philosophy* 24 (1949), 23
Summers, R. S. (ed.), *More Essays in Legal Philosophy*, Oxford: Oxford University Press, 1971

Taylor, Michael, *Community, Anarchy and Liberty*, Cambridge: Cambridge University Press, 1982

Thoreau, H. D., "Civil Disobedience," *Walden and Civil Disobedience*, ed. S. Paul, Boston: Houghton Mifflin Co., 1960

Williams, Bernard, "A Critique of Utilitarianism" in Smart and Williams, *Utilitarianism – For and Against*

  Moral Luck, Cambridge: Cambridge University Press 1981

  "Practical Necessity" in Williams, *Moral Luck*

Wolff, Robert Paul, *In Defense of Anarchism*, New York: Harper, 1970

Woozley, A. D., *Law and Obedience: The Arguments of Plato's Crito*, London: Duckworth, 1979

Index